I0737604
9781681985053

NIKON
D500
POCKET GUIDE

TABLE OF CONTENTS

01 PRE-SHOOT CHECKLIST

02 BUTTONS, DIALS, AND SCREENS

CAMERA BODY TOP 2
CAMERA BODY BACK 3
CAMERA BODY FRONT 5
CAMERA BODY BOTTOM 6
VIEWFINDER DISPLAY 7
CONTROL PANEL 9

03 ESSENTIAL MODES AND SETTINGS

EXPOSURE MODES 10
METERING MODES 10
EXPOSURE COMPENSATION 11
FOCUS MODES 11
FOCUS AREAS 12
RELEASE MODES 13
WHITE BALANCE 14
FILE FORMATS 15

04 OTHER HELPFUL SETTINGS

PICTURE CONTROLS 16
FLASH MODES 17
CUSTOM WHITE BALANCE (LIVE VIEW) 18
COLOR SPACE 18
HIGHLIGHT WARNINGS (BLINKIES) 19
NOISE REDUCTION 19
AUTO ISO 19
VIRTUAL HORIZON 20
ACTIVE D-LIGHTING 20
BRACKETING 21
RESET CAMERA 22
WIRELESS CONNECTION (SNAPBRIDGE) 22

05 STEP-BY-STEP SHOOTING INSTRUCTIONS

MULTIPLE EXPOSURES 23
HDR 24
TIME-LAPSE MOVIES 24
INTERVAL TIMER PHOTOGRAPHY 25

06 TYPICAL SHOOTING SCENARIOS

PORTRAIT 26
GROUP PORTRAIT 27
LANDSCAPE 29
FREEZE ACTION 30
SHOWING MOTION—PANNING 31
LOW-LIGHT ACTION 32
LONG EXPOSURE 33
MACRO/CLOSE-UP 34

01 PRE-SHOOT CHECKLIST

Check these settings before you head out with your camera!

SETTING	MY PREFERRED SETTING
☑ Exposure Mode	....
☑ White Balance Setting	....
☑ ISO Setting	....
☑ Focus Mode	....
☑ Focus Area	....
☑ Release Mode	....
☑ Metering Mode	....
☑ Bracketing: On/Off	....
☑ File Format: JPEG, RAW, or RAW+JPEG	....
☑ Highlight Warning (Blinkies): On/Off	....
☑ Picture Control	....
☑ Vibration Reduction: On/Off	....
☑ Battery Fully Charged and In Camera	....
☑ Memory Card Formatted and In Camera	....

02 BUTTONS, DIALS, AND SCREENS

CAMERA BODY TOP

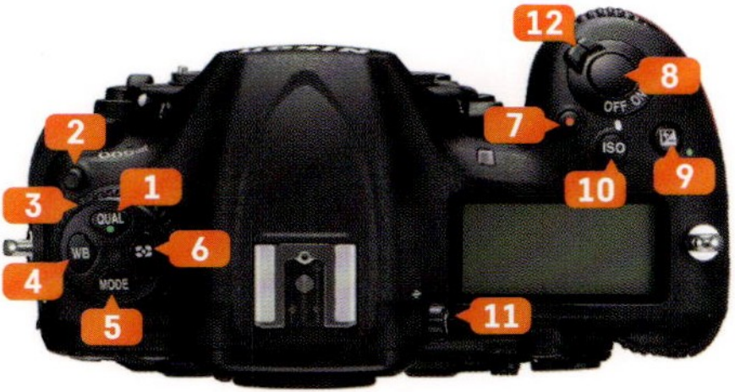

1. QUAL Button: Press, then rotate Main Command dial to change image quality between RAW and JPEG.

2. Release Mode Dial Lock Release: Press to release Release Mode dial.

3. Release Mode Dial: Set Release mode.

4. WB (White Balance) Button: Press, then rotate Main Command dial to change White Balance.

5. MODE Button: Press, then rotate Main Command dial to change Exposure mode between P (Program Auto), A (Aperture Priority), S (Shutter Speed Priority), and M (Manual).

6. Metering Mode Button: Press, then rotate Main Command dial to change Metering mode.

7. Movie Record Button: Start and end recording when shooting video.

8. Shutter Release Button: Press halfway to activate autofocus and all the way to take photo.

9. Exposure Compensation Button: Press, then rotate Main Command dial to adjust exposure compensation.

10. ISO Button: Press, then rotate Main Command dial to adjust ISO.

11. Diopter Adjustment Control: Pull out and turn to adjust diopter in viewfinder.

12. Power Switch: Turn camera on and off.

CAMERA BODY BACK

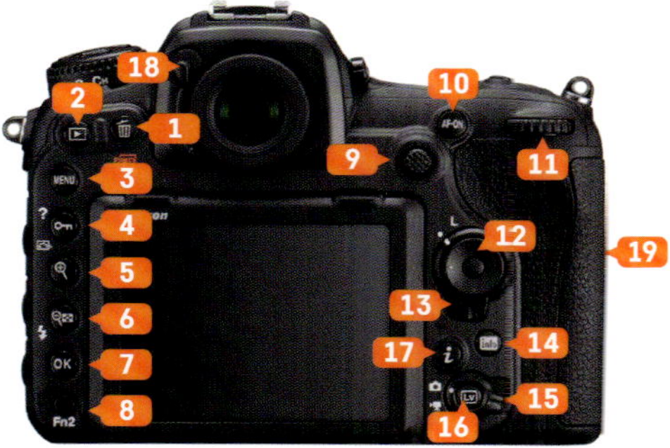

1. Trash Button: Delete current image on LCD.

2. Playback Button: Show last image taken on LCD.

3. MENU Button: Opens/closes the menu system.

4. Image Protect/Picture Control/Menu Information Button: Press to protect current image on the LCD from deletion / Open Picture Control Menu / Press for contextual menu information when "?" on bottom left of LCD.

5. Zoom In Button: Zoom in on current image shown on LCD.

6. **Zoom Out/Flash Button:** Zoom out on current image shown on LCD / Set flash settings.

7. **OK Button:** Use to select current option in menu mode.

8. **Fn2 Button:** Assignable Function button set in the Custom Settings Menu: F Controls.

9. **Sub-Selector:** Use to select autofocus point(s).

10. **AF-ON Button:** Press to engage autofocus.

11. **Main Command Dial:** Use to adjust camera settings.

12. **Multi Selector:** Use to navigate menus or select AF point.

13. **Focus Selector Lock:** Locks the Multi Selector so current focus point cannot be changed.

14. **Info Button:** Shows or hides Information Display.

15. **Live View Selector:** Switches between Still Live View and Movie Live View modes.

16. **Live View Button:** Engages the selected Live View mode.

17. **i Button:** Opens contextual menu depending on shooting mode (Live View, Movie, Still).

18. **Eyepiece Shutter Lever:** Close this shutter when taking photos without your eye to the viewfinder in order to prevent light from entering through the viewfinder.

19. **Memory Card Slots and Cover:** The upper slot is for XQD cards and the lower slot is for SD cards.

CAMERA BODY FRONT

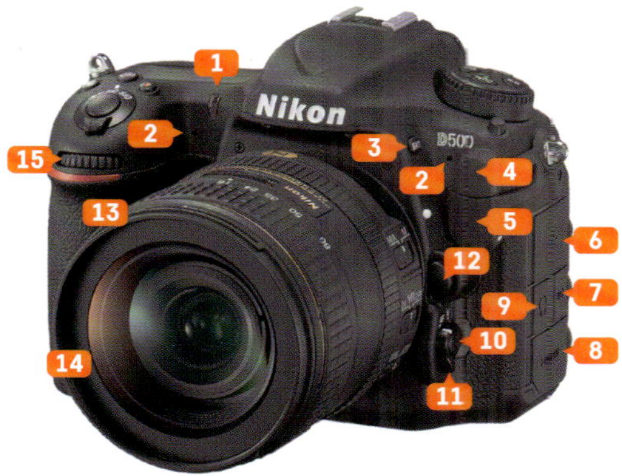

1. **Self-Timer Lamp:** Blinks when self-timer is active.
2. **Stereo Microphones:** Records audio when recording movies.
3. **BKT Button:** Press, then turn Main Command dial to set bracketing.
4. **Flash Sync Terminal (under rubber cover):** Use with flash sync cord.
5. **10 Pin Remote Terminal (under cover):** Use with Nikon 10 pin accessories.
6. **USB Connector (under cover):** Connect to USB devices.
7. **Microphone Connector (under cover):** Connect external microphone to camera.
8. **HDMI Connector (under cover):** Connect HDMI cable.
9. **Headphone Jack (under cover):** Connect headphones to camera.
10. **AF Mode Button:** Press, then rotate Main Command dial (to change Focus mode) or Sub-Command dial (to change Focus Area mode).

11. Focus Mode Selector: Switch between autofocus and manual focus.

12. Lens Release Button: Press button and rotate lens to remove lens from camera body.

13. Pv (Preview) Button: Assignable button with default as Depth of Field Preview.

14. Fn1 Button: Assignable Function button set in the Custom Settings Menu: F Controls.

15. Sub-Command Dial: Use to adjust camera settings.

CAMERA BODY BOTTOM

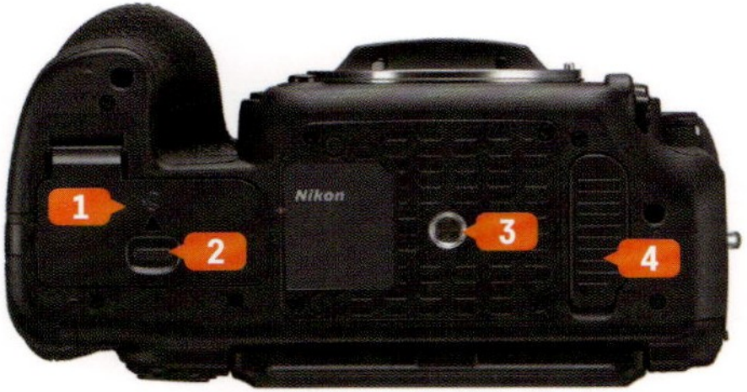

1. Battery Chamber Cover: Open to access the camera battery.

2. Battery Chamber Cover Latch: Use to open the battery cover and make sure it is locked after closing cover.

3. Tripod Socket: Standard tripod socket used to attach a tripod or monopod.

4. Contact Cover for Optional MB-D17 Battery Pack: Remove and store in the MB-D17 when using the optional battery pack.

VIEWFINDER DISPLAY

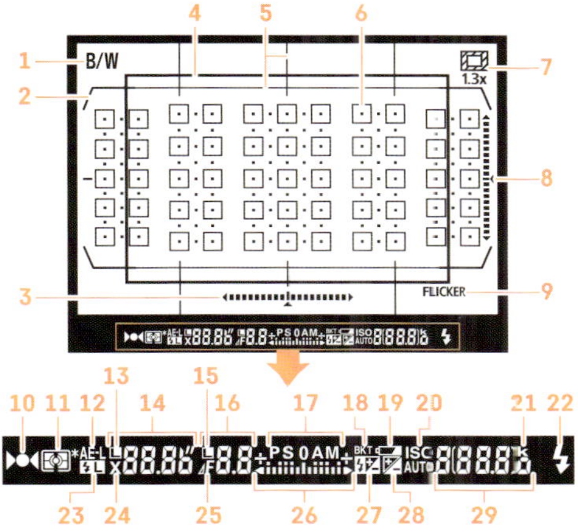

1. **Monochrome Indicator:** Present when using the Monochrome Picture Control.
2. **AF Area Brackets:** Shows autofocus area.
3. **Roll Indicator:** Shows camera's side-to-side tilt.
4. **1.3 Crop Outline:** Illuminates when using the 1.3 crop.
5. **Framing Grid:** Shows frame.
6. **Focus Points:** There are 153 focus points, 55 of which can be selected by the user.
7. **1.3 Crop Indicator:** Signifies using the 1.3 crop
8. **Pitch Indicator:** Shows the front-to-back camera tilt.
9. **Flicker Detection:** Shows when flicker reduction is on.

10. Focus Indicator: The circle illuminates if the subject is in focus; the arrows illuminate if the subject is not in focus.
11. Metering Mode: Displays the current Metering mode.
12. AE Lock: Illuminates when AE lock is active.
13. Shutter Speed Lock Icon: Illuminates if shutter speed lock is active.
14. Shutter Speed: Shows the current shutter speed.
15. Aperture Lock Icon: Illuminates if aperture lock is active.
16. Aperture: Shows the current aperture.
17. Exposure Mode: Shows the current Exposure mode.
18. Bracketing Indicator: Illuminates when bracketing is active.
19. Low Battery Warning: Indicates low battery level.
20. ISO/Auto ISO Indicator: Shows if ISO /Auto ISO is being used.
21. K: Shows when memory for over 1000 images remains.
22. Flash Ready Indicator: Illuminates when the flash is ready to fire.
23. FV Lock Indicator: Illuminates when Flash Value (FV) is locked.
24. Flash Sync Indicator: Shows when the shutter speed is fixed to the flash sync speed.
25. Aperture Stop Indicator: Shows aperture.
26. Exposure Indicator/Exposure Compensation Display: Shows the current exposure value or the exposure value with any exposure compensation applied.
27. Flash Compensation Indicator: Shows when there is any Flash Compensation applied.
28. Exposure Compensation Indicator: Shows when there is any Exposure Compensation applied.
29. Number of Exposures Remaining/ISO/Other: A contextual display that shows one of the following: the number of exposures remaining, the number of shots remaining until the buffer fills, ISO, Preset WB recoding, Active D-Lighting amount, AF-Area mode, Exposure Compensation value, Flash Compensation value, PC mode indicator.

CONTROL PANEL

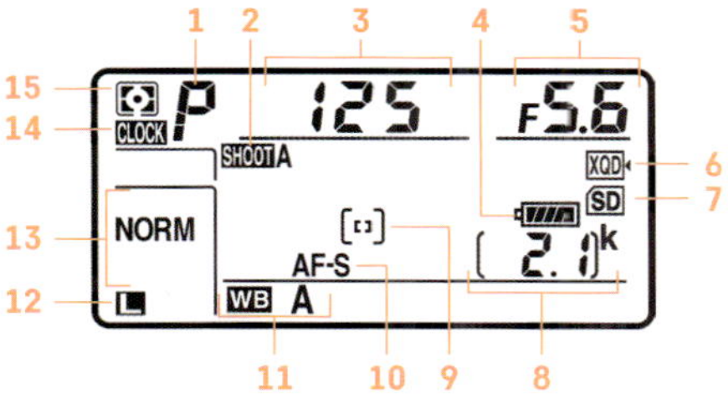

1. **Exposure Mode:** Shows the current Exposure mode.
2. **Photo Shooting Menu Bank:** Shows current shooting bank: A or B.
3. **Shutter Speed:** Shows the current shutter speed.
4. **Battery Life:** Shows the battery life. Will flash when battery is dead and camera can no longer take photos.
5. **Aperture:** Shows the current aperture value.
6. **XQD Card:** Shows XQD when an XQD card is in the camera.
7. **SD Card:** Shows SD when an SD card is in the camera.
8. **Remaining Exposures:** Shows the number of remaining exposures.
9. **AF-Area Mode:** Shows the current autofocus area.
10. **AF Mode:** Shows the current autofocus mode.
11. **White Balance:** Shows the current White Balance setting.
12. **Image Size:** Shows the Image Size when shooting JPEG or TIFF file types.
13. **Image Quality:** Shows the current Image Quality setting.
14. **Clock:** Flashes if the clock needs to be reset.
15. **Metering Mode:** Shows the current Metering mode.

Note: When there is no battery or the battery is dead, the Control Panel display will dim.

03 ESSENTIAL MODES AND SETTINGS

MODE EXPOSURE MODES

Press the MODE button and rotate the Main Command dial.

P (Programmed Auto): Camera sets shutter speed and aperture based on metering info and current ISO.

S (Shutter Speed Priority): You set shutter speed and camera sets aperture based on metering info and current ISO. Shutter speed can be set between 30 sec.–1/8000 sec.

A (Aperture Priority): You set aperture and camera sets shutter speed based on metering info and current ISO. Range of apertures depends on the lens.

M (Manual): You set both shutter speed and aperture. Can set shutter speed to Bulb mode for long exposures.

METERING MODES

Press Metering Mode button and rotate Main Command dial.

Matrix: Uses whole frame along with lens information (color, distance) from G, E, and D lenses to determine the best exposure. Best for most situations.

Center-Weighted: Analyzes the entire frame but gives more weight to the center of frame.

Spot: Measures area under current focus point (2.5% of the frame).

Highlight-Weighted: Camera uses settings that keep detail in the brightest highlights.

EXPOSURE COMPENSATION

Press Exposure Compensation button and turn Main Command dial to adjust exposure from −5 (darker) to +5 (lighter) stops in 1/3-stop increments.

Note: In M exposure mode, Exposure Compensation will change exposure indicator but not shutter speed or aperture.

FOCUS MODES

Push center of AF Mode button and turn Main Command dial.

AF-S (Single-Servo AutoFocus): Focus starts when Shutter Release button is pressed and locks when focus is achieved. Best for stationary subjects.

AF-C (Continuous-Servo AutoFocus): Focus starts when Shutter Release button is pressed halfway and continues to focus until photo is taken. Best for moving subjects.

AF-F (Full-Time-Servo AutoFocus): Available in Live View only. Focus tracks subject continuously until Shutter Release button is pressed halfway down. Can really drain the battery.
M (Manual Focus): Focusing is accomplished by turning the focusing ring on the lens barrel. Some lenses have a M/A—M switch on lens; set to M.

FOCUS AREAS

Push center of AF Mode button and turn Sub-Command dial.
Single-Point AF: Uses single point for critical focus.
Dynamic-Area AF: Can select 25, 72, or 153 points, and camera tries to keep moving subject in focus (AF-C only).
Auto-Area AF: Camera focuses on closest thing, but faces are given priority and camera tries to focus on people over other objects.
3D-Tracking: Select initial focus point and then camera uses color and distance information from lens to keep focus on that subject even as it moves (AF-C only).
Group-Area AF: A group of points is used as a larger single focus point. Easier to use but can be less accurate than a single point.

Live View Only:

Choose from among these autofocus options when you're in Live View mode.

Face-Priority AF: Keeps focus on any faces.

Wide-Area AF: Wider area used for focusing. Move focus area with Multi Selector.

Normal-Area AF: Smaller area for more critical focusing. Move focus area with Multi Selector.

Subject-Tracking AF: Camera tracks subjects moving in frame.

RELEASE MODES

Press Release Mode Dial Lock Release, then turn Release Mode dial to desired setting.

S (Single Frame): Takes a single shot every time Shutter Release button is pressed.

CL (Continuous Low): Takes between 1–9 frames per second (FPS) as long as you press Shutter Release button.

CH (Continuous High): Takes up to 10 FPS for as long as you press Shutter Release button.

Q (Quiet Shutter-Release): Mirror does not return down until pressure is removed from Shutter Release button; camera will not beep when focus is locked.

QC (Quiet Continuous Shutter-Release): Three frames taken in succession in quiet mode.

Self-Timer: When Shutter Release button is pressed fully, camera waits a set time before taking photo. Amount of delay and number of images taken can be set in Custom Settings Menu: C Timers/AE Lock.

MUP (Mirror Up): Press Shutter Release button once to raise mirror up and out of the way. Press Shutter Release button a second time to take photo.

WHITE BALANCE

Press the WB button and rotate Main Command dial.

Auto setting is best for most situations. White balance can be set to shift colors warmer or cooler, or keep them accurate. Other settings are all matched to different lighting types. Pick type of lighting used to illuminate scene for truest colors. Quickest way to see effect of white balance selection: open Live View and cycle through WB choices while looking at LCD.

FILE FORMATS

Press the QUAL button and rotate Main Command dial to cycle through the file options.

RAW (NEF): The RAW data from the image sensor is recorded each time a photo is taken.

RAW (NEF)/JPEG: The camera saves two files each time the Shutter Release button is pressed: a RAW file and a JPEG file You can decide the size of the JPEG (Fine, Normal, or Basic).

JPEG: The camera saves a JPEG file each time the Shutter Release button is pressed. You can decide the size of the JPEG (Fine, Normal, or Basic).

TIFF: The camera saves a single TIFF file each time a photo is taken. The TIFF file is supported by most image-editing software.

Note: The JPEG files can be saved as either regular files or compressed files (the compressed options are marked with a star).

04 OTHER HELPFUL SETTINGS

PICTURE CONTROLS

Press Picture Control button (with key on it, under MENU button) and select the desired Picture Control. Press OK, or press right on Multi Selector to adjust Picture Control. Allows you to adjust settings for JPEG images. Adjustable settings are Sharpening, Clarity, Contrast, Saturation, Brightness, and Hue. Seven preset picture controls can all be adjusted: **SD (Standard), NL (Neutral), VI (Vivid), MC (Monochrome), PT (Portrait), LS (Landscape), FL (Flat).** You can also create custom controls in the Manage Picture Control menu (within the Photo Shooting Menu). Monochrome images can have a Yellow, Orange, Red, or Green filter applied. ***Note:*** If shooting RAW, Picture Controls can be helpful when looking at LCD in order to evaluate the "look" you want.

FLASH MODES

Press Zoom Out/Flash button and rotate the Main Command dial.

Front Curtain Sync: Default. When using P or A exposure mode, camera uses shutter speed between 1/60–1/250 sec. (1/60–1/8000 sec. when Auto FP High Speed Sync is selected).

Red-Eye Reduction: Flash fires twice: first burst is so that subject's pupils close, reducing the red-eye. Not good for moving subjects.

Red-Eye Reduction with Slow Sync: Combines red-eye reduction pre-flash and slow sync for better portraits taken when you want ambient light in photo.

Slow Sync: Flash is used in conjunction with slower shutter speeds to allow ambient light into photo. Only available in P and A exposure modes.

Rear-Curtain Sync: Flash fires at end of exposure, creating more natural looking light trails if subject is moving. Only available in S and M exposure modes.

Flash Off: Flash does not fire.

K CUSTOM WHITE BALANCE (LIVE VIEW)

Custom White Balance is useful when shooting under mixed lighting to get the best color.

1. Turn on Live View (rotate the Live View Selector to Live View, then press the Live View button) and aim camera at scene, then press WB button and rotate the Main Command dial until PRE is displayed.

2. With WB button still pressed, rotate the Sub-Command dial until the WB preset you want to change (d1 – d6) is selected, then release WB button.

3. To access direct measurement mode, press WB button again and hold until PRE icon at top right of screen flashes. Move white balance target around using Multi Selector until it is over the area where you want to measure light. Press the center of the Multi Selector to measure the white balance.

4. Press the WB button to exit the direct measurement mode.

COLOR SPACE

Photo Shooting Menu > Color Space

sRGB: Smaller color space. Best when images are used directly from camera.

Adobe RGB: Larger color space. Best used when images will be edited with post-processing software.

HIGHLIGHT WARNINGS (BLINKIES)

Playback Menu > Playback Display Options > Highlights

Shows pure white areas blinking with a black border during playback. Useful to know if areas are being overexposed so that you can adjust exposure and shoot again.

NOISE REDUCTION

Photo Shooting Menu > Long Exposure NR

Reduces noise in images with 1 sec. or longer shutter speeds. Doubles time needed to save image to card. Affects both RAW and JPEG images.

Photo Shooting Menu > High ISO NR

Reduces noise in images taken at high ISO settings. Use Normal for default, Low for less noise reduction, and High for more. Only affects JPEG images.

AUTO ISO

Photo Shooting Menu > ISO Sensitivity Settings > Auto ISO Sensitivity Control

Maximum Sensitivity: Highest ISO camera will use.

Maximum Sensitivity with Flash: Highest ISO camera will use when also using a flash.

Minimum Shutter Speed: Slowest shutter speed camera will use before increasing ISO. If Auto is selected, camera picks shutter speed depending on focal length of lens.

VIRTUAL HORIZON

Setup Menu > Virtual Horizon

A virtual horizon (level) shows on the LCD, allowing you to adjust the camera until it is properly aligned. Useful for shooting landscapes.

ACTIVE D-LIGHTING

Photo Shooting Menu > Active D-Lighting

Use when shooting JPEGs to help preserve detail that can be lost in both the darkest and brightest parts of a high-contrast image. ***Note:*** Can cause image issues such as banding and noise at higher ISO settings.

BKT BRACKETING

Photo Shooting Menu > Auto Bracketing Set

Auto Bracketing is used to take a set of images where exposure, flash power, white balance, or Active D-Lighting is changed slightly between each frame. You can set the camera to whichever option you would like to bracket.

Exposure (AE) & Flash: Changes the exposure and the flash power.

Exposure (AE Only): Changes the exposure.

Flash Only: Changes the flash power.

WB Bracketing: Changes the white balance.

ADL Bracketing: Changes the amount of the Active D-Lighting applied.

Press the BKT button, then rotate the Main Command dial to choose the number of photos in the bracket, then turn the Sub-Command dial to set either the exposure/flash increment, the white balance adjustment, or the Active D-Lighting adjustment.

Note: When the number of photos is set to 0, bracketing is turned off.

RESET CAMERA

Hold the QUAL button and Exposure Compensation button down simultaneously for more than 2 seconds.

Camera settings reset to factory defaults. Control panel turns off for a moment while camera is reset. The two buttons used both have green dots near them.

WIRELESS CONNECTION (SNAPBRIDGE)

Use Nikon SnapBridge app on your smartphone or tablet to connect D500 to device.

Allows for wireless downloading of images and remote control of camera via Bluetooth.

05 STEP-BY-STEP SHOOTING INSTRUCTIONS

MULTIPLE EXPOSURES

Create in-camera multiple exposures:

1. Select Photo Shooting Menu > Multiple Exposure, and press right on the Multi Selector.
2. Choose the Multiple Exposure mode:

   On (series): Takes multiple exposures until Off is selected.

   On (single): Takes one multiple exposure.

   Off: Turns multiple exposures off.
3. Select the Number of Shots to combine.
4. Pick the Overlay mode:

   Add: The images are combined without any modification.

   Average: Before the images are combined the gain for each image is divided by the total number of images to create a proper exposure.

   Lighten: Camera uses only lightest pixels of each image to create an overall light image.

   Darken: Camera uses only darkest pixels of each image to create an overall dark image.
5. Compose the photo, focus, and shoot.

HDR HDR

Combine two JPEG images to reduce the contrast and improve tonal range:

1. Select Photo Shooting Menu > HDR (High Dynamic Range), and press right on the Multi Selector.
2. Choose HDR Mode and decide to shoot either a single occurrence (On [single photo]) or a series (On [series]), which will continue to shoot HDR until you select Off in HDR Mode.
3. Pick the Exposure Differential between two photos, as well as the Smoothing.
4. Compose the photo, focus, and shoot.

TIME-LAPSE MOVIES

Create a time-lapse movie in-camera:

1. Select Movie Shooting Menu > Time-Lapse Movie, and press right on the Multi Selector.
2. Select the Interval: the time between each photo. Set in minutes and seconds.
3. Select the Shooting Time: how long to shoot (up to 7 hours and 59 minutes).

4. Choose whether you want to use Exposure Smoothing. When On, it automatically tries to smooth any big changes in the exposure.

5. Select Start and press OK to start shooting.

INTVL INTERVAL TIMER PHOTOGRAPHY

Set the camera to take a series of photos over a period of time:

1. Select Photo Shooting Menu > Interval Timer Shooting, and press right on the Multi Selector.
2. Set Start Options to begin either in 3 seconds (Now) or at least 1 minute in future (Choose Start Day and Start Time).
3. Set the Interval between photos (Hours/Minutes/Seconds).
4. Set the number of intervals and the number of shots per interval (No. of Intervals x Shots/Interval).
5. Turn Exposure Smoothing On or Off.
6. Select Start and press OK.

06 TYPICAL SHOOTING SCENARIOS

SHOOTING SCENARIO
PORTRAIT

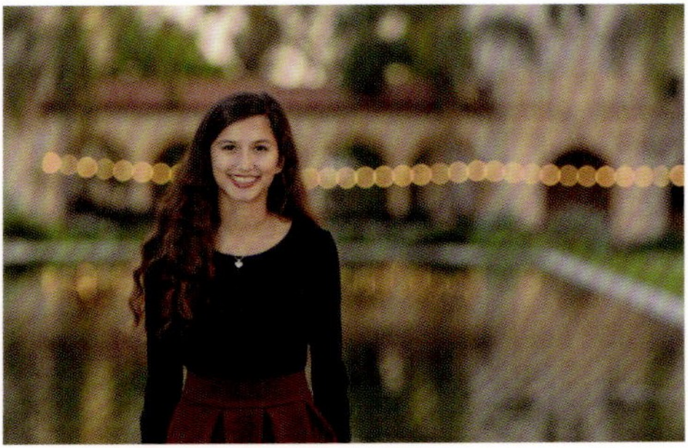

KEY PRINCIPLES

- The key to a portrait like this is shallow depth of field. So shoot in **APERTURE PRIORITY** mode and start with the lowest aperture your lens offers (such as **f/2.8 or f/4**).
- Remember to **focus on the eyes**.
- If the image is too dark or too light, use **EXPOSURE COMPENSATION** to adjust the brightness level.

- If the image is blurry from a slow shutter speed, **raise the ISO** to increase your sensor's sensitivity to light thus allowing for a faster shutter speed.
- Remember to use a **focal length of 50mm or greater** so that you don't distort your subject's face.

SHOOTING SCENARIO
GROUP PORTRAIT

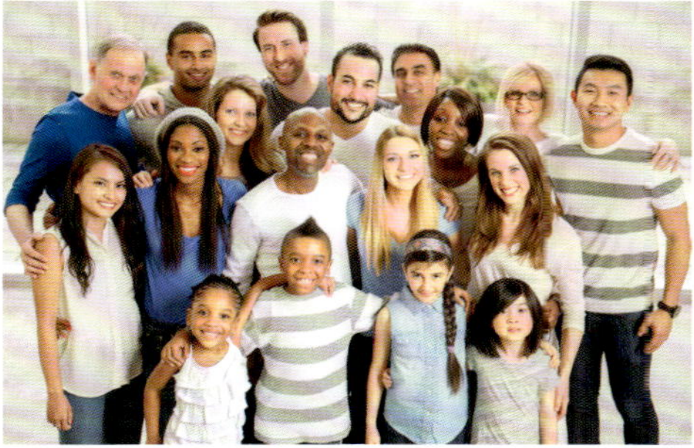

KEY PRINCIPLES

- In order to get everyone in focus, you need a deep depth of field. So shoot in **APERTURE PRIORITY** mode and set the aperture between **f/8–f/16**.

- **Focus on the person in the middle of the group**. Check focus using the LCD, but view it at 100% and check faces in the front and back rows. If anyone is out of focus, use a smaller aperture for deeper depth of field.
- Use **MATRIX METERING** to account for the light in the entire scene.
- **Arrange the group so they can all see you** (and you can see them).
- Use **EXPOSURE COMPENSATION** if the image is too bright or too dark.
- If image is blurry, **raise the ISO** to allow the camera to use a faster shutter speed.

LANDSCAPE

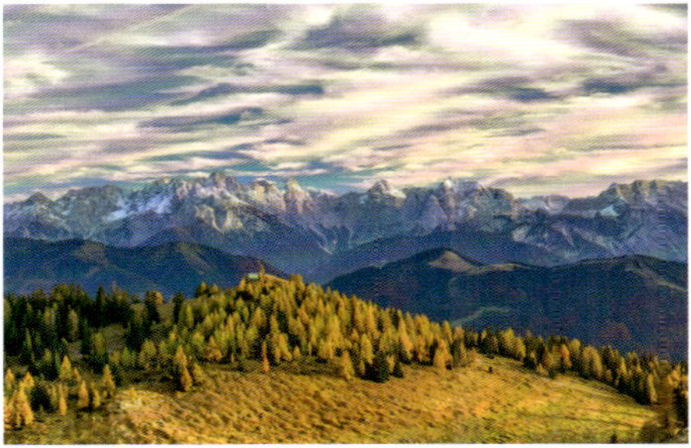

KEY PRINCIPLES

- Shoot in **APERTURE PRIORITY** to control depth of field, and start with **f/16** to ensure deep depth of field.
- Use a **tripod** to eliminate camera movement. Whenever your camera is on a tripod, also make sure that **VIBRATION REDUCTION** is turned off.
- Use **MATRIX METERING** mode and **SINGLE AUTOFOCUS (AF-S)** focus mode.
- **Set the ISO to a low setting (100–200)** to avoid any digital noise.
- Shoot in **RAW** so that you have the most available information when editing later.
- Consider **BRACKETING** your exposures.

SHOOTING SCENARIO

FREEZE ACTION

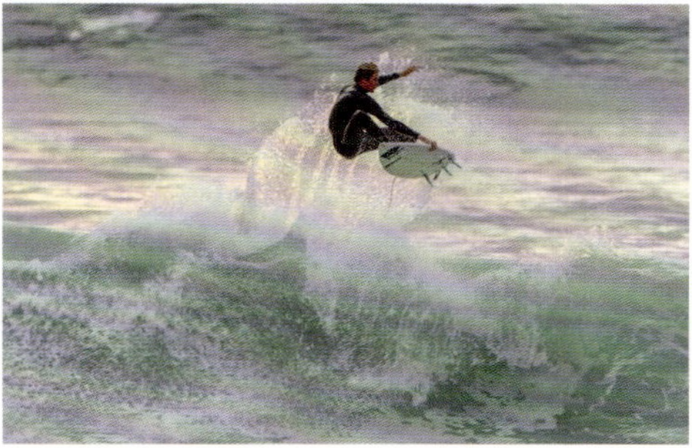

KEY PRINCIPLES

- Use **SHUTTER PRIORITY** mode and set the shutter speed to a value that will freeze the action. The appropriate shutter speed depends on your subject and its movement, but could be anywhere between **1/500–1/8000 sec**.
- Use **CONTINUOUS AUTOFOCUS (AF-C)** so that the camera keeps focusing as the subject moves.
- Try the **GROUP-AREA AF** setting to make it easier to maintain focus on the moving subject.
- If the image is dark or blurry, **raise the ISO** or try Auto ISO to automatically have the camera adjust the ISO as needed.

SHOOTING SCENARIO

SHOWING MOTION—PANNING

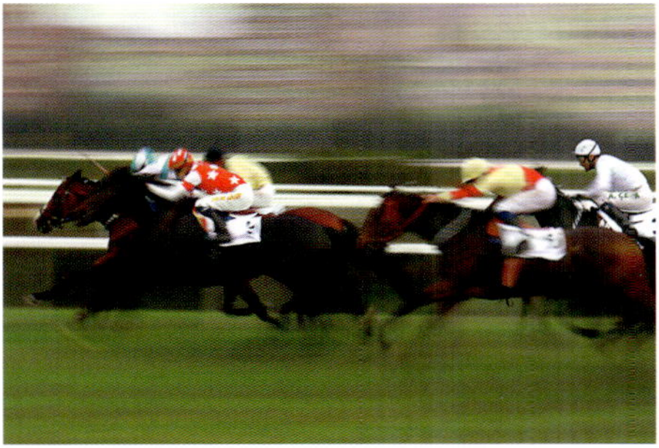

KEY PRINCIPLES

- Shoot in **SHUTTER PRIORITY** mode and use a slow-enough shutter speed to allow for the subject to move during the exposure.
- **Follow the subject** across the frame as you shoot.
- Try **LIVE VIEW**, which allows you to see the subject during the exposure.
- Use **CONTINUOUS AUTOFOCUS (AF-C)**, as well as **GROUP-AREA AF**.

SHOOTING SCENARIO
LOW-LIGHT ACTION

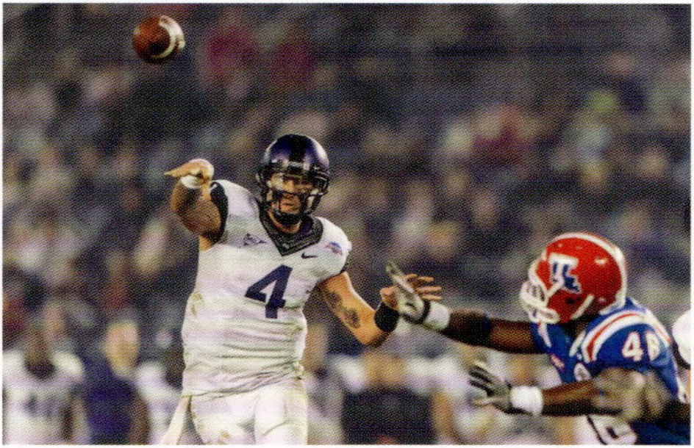

KEY PRINCIPLES

- Shoot in **APERTURE PRIORITY** mode and use a wide aperture such as **f/2.8 or f/4**.
- Use **SPOT METERING** and meter on the subject's face.
- Use **CONTINUOUS AUTOFOCUS (AF-C)** and a single AF point.
- **Set the ISO to 1600 or higher**, depending on the amount of available light.
- If the image is blurry, **increase the ISO** to allow for a faster shutter speed.

SHOOTING SCENARIO

LONG EXPOSURE

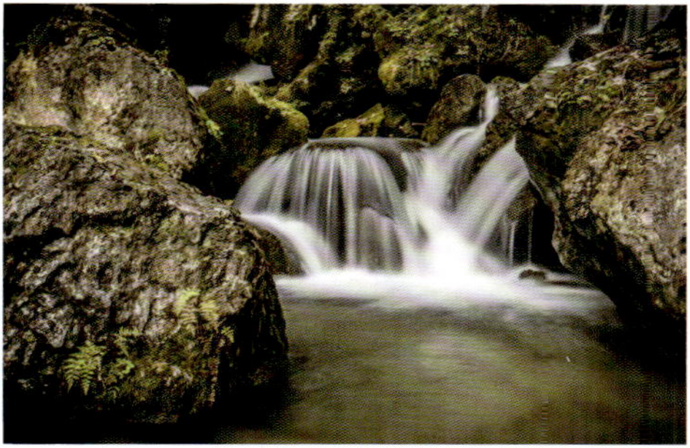

KEY PRINCIPLES

- Use **MANUAL** exposure mode, which allows you to use the **BULB** shutter speed for long exposures.
- **Use a tripod** to keep the camera stable. Turn off any **VIBRATION REDUCTION** setting.
- Use **SINGLE AUTOFOCUS (AF-S)** or try manual focus if the camera is having a hard time locking on focus.
- Use a **low ISO** (100–400) and **shoot RAW** to ensure a high-quality file.
- Use a **cable release** with a lock to avoid touching (shaking) the camera.

SHOOTING SCENARIO

MACRO/CLOSE-UP

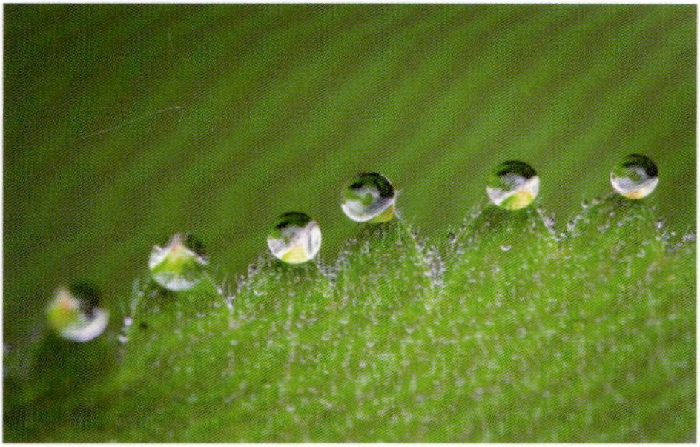

KEY PRINCIPLES

- Shoot in **APERTURE PRIORITY** mode and use a small aperture to ensure you achieve enough depth of field (this image was shot at f/13).
- Use **MATRIX METERING** to analyze the light in the entire frame.
- A **tripod** is very useful for keeping the camera steady.
- Use **MANUAL FOCUS** and **zoom in** to confirm your focus is tack-sharp.
- Try using a dedicated **macro lens** or **close-up filters** to make sure you can achieve sharp focus when you're so close to the subject.

5. **Headphone Connector (under cover, right side):** Connect headphones to camera.
6. **USB Connector (under cover, right side):** Connect to USB devices.
7. **HDMI Connector (under cover, right side):** Connect HDMI cable.
8. **Accessory Terminal (under cover, right side):** Connect remote.
9. **Microphone Connector (under cover, right side):** Connect microphone to camera.

CAMERA BODY BOTTOM

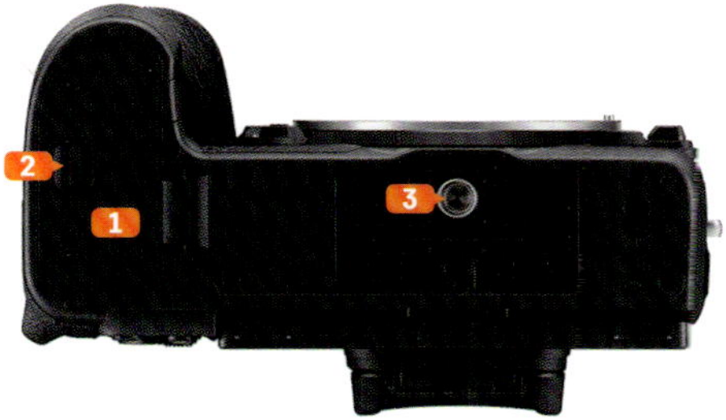

1. **Battery Chamber Cover:** Open to access the camera battery.
2. **Battery Chamber Cover Latch:** Use to open the battery cover. Make sure it is locked after closing cover.
3. **Tripod Socket:** Standard tripod socket for attaching a tripod or monopod.

VIEWFINDER DISPLAY

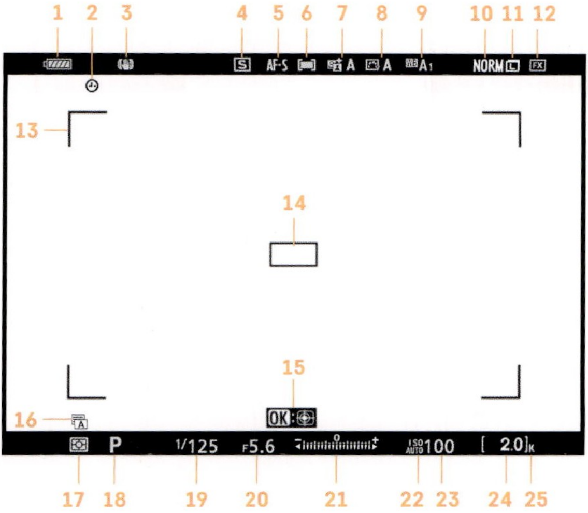

1. Battery Indicator: Displays amount of power left.

2. Clock Not Set Indicator: Flashes if clock is not set.

3. Vibration Reduction Indicator: Indicates if Vibration Reduction is active (On/Sports), not shown if VR is off.

4. Release Mode: Shows the current Release mode: S (Single Frame), L (Continuous Low), H (Continuous High), Self-Timer.

6. **Active D-Lighting:** Shows the status of Active D-Lighting.
7. **Picture Control:** Shows the current Picture Control.
8. **White Balance:** Shows the current White Balance.
9. **Image Area:** Shows the current image area: FX for full screen and DX for cropped area.
10. **Image Size:** Shows the current image size: Large, Medium, or Small, for both RAW and JPEG.
11. **Image Quality:** Shows the current image quality: RAW, RAW+JPEG, or JPEG.
12. ***i* Icon:** Tap the *i* icon to open the *i* menu.
13. **Exposure Indicator/Exposure Compensation Display:** Shows the current exposure; shows if there is any exposure compensation being applied.
14. **K:** Shows when memory for over 1000 images remains.
15. **Number of Remaining Exposures:** Displays the number of exposures that can be taken based on memory card's available space.
16. **ISO:** Shows the current ISO.
17. **ISO Sensitivity Indicator:** Shows if Auto ISO is engaged.
18. **Subject-Tracking AF:** Shows when Subject-Tracking AF is active.
19. **Aperture:** Shows the current aperture.
20. **Shutter Speed:** Shows the current shutter speed.
21. **Metering:** Shows the current Metering mode.
22. **Battery Indicator:** Displays amount of power left.
23. **Shutter Type:** Shows which type of shutter is being used: Auto, Mechanical, or Electronic Front Curtain.
24. **Vibration Reduction Indicator:** Indicates if Vibration Reduction is active (On/Sports), not shown if VR is off.
25. **Touch Shooting:** Shows if touch shooting is enabled.
26. **Clock Not Set Indicator:** Flashes if clock is not set.
27. **AF-Area Brackets:** Shows the current AF-Area.

VIEWFINDER DISPLAY (MOVIE)

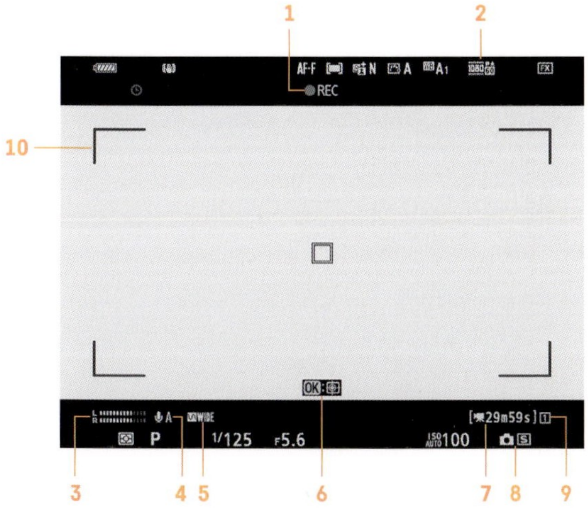

1. Recording Indicator/Recording Disabled: Shows when movies are being recorded; shows when movies cannot be recorded.

2. Frame Size and Rate/Image Quality: Shows the current frame size and rate; shows image quality for still images.

3. Sound Level: Shows current sound levels. If red, then it's too high and the mic sensitivity needs to be reduced.

4. Microphone Sensitivity: The sensitivity can be set for Auto or 1–20 (higher value is more sensitive).

5. **Frequency Response:** Shows current mode (Wide Range or Vocal Range).
6. **Subject Tracking:** Shows when subject tracking is turned on.
7. **Time Remaining:** Shows the amount of time remaining until memory card will become full or maximum length of movie is reached.
8. **Release Mode (for still photography):** The mode used to take still images while movie is being recorded.
9. **Destination:** Shows which card (1 or 2) the movie will be saved to.
10. **AF-Area Brackets:** Shows the current AF-Area.

MONITOR DISPLAY (MOVIE)

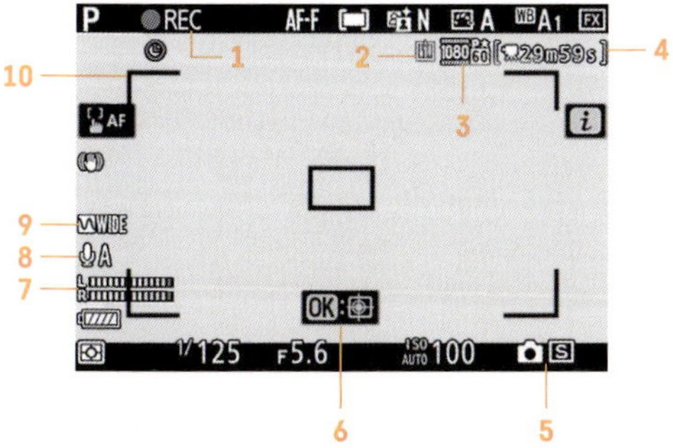

1. Recording Indicator/Recording Disabled: Shows when movies are being recorded; shows when movies cannot be recorded.

2. Destination: Show which card (1 or 2) the movie will be saved to.

3. Frame Size and Rate/Image Quality: Shows the current frame size and rate; shows image quality for still images.

4. Time Remaining: Shows the amount of time remaining until memory card will become full or maximum length of movie is reached.

5. Release Mode (for still photography): The mode used to take still images while movie is being recorded.

6. Subject Tracking: Shows when subject tracking is turned on.

7. Sound Level: Shows current sound levels. If red, then it's too high and the mic sensitivity needs to be reduced.

8. **Microphone Sensitivity:** The sensitivity can be set for Auto or 1–20 (higher value is more sensitive).

9. **Frequency Response:** Shows current mode (Wide Range or Vocal Range).

10. **AF-Area Brackets:** Shows the current AF-Area.

03 ESSENTIAL MODES AND SETTINGS

MODE SHOOTING MODES

Press the Mode Dial Lock Release and rotate the Mode dial to choose the Shooting mode.

Auto (Auto): Point-and-shoot mode where the camera sets the exposure.

P (Programmed Auto): Camera sets shutter speed and aperture based on metering info and current ISO.

S (Shutter Priority): You set shutter speed, and camera sets aperture based on metering info and current ISO. Shutter speed can be set between 30 sec.–1/8000 sec.

A (Aperture Priority): You set aperture, and camera sets shutter speed based on metering info and current ISO. Range of apertures depends on the lens.

M (Manual): You set both shutter speed and aperture. Can set shutter speed to Bulb mode for long exposures.

U1, U2, U3 (User Settings): You can assign frequently used settings to these three modes for quick recall.

METERING MODES

Press the *i* button and use the Multi Selector to select the Metering icon. Then rotate the Main Command dial to select from the following Metering modes.

Matrix: Uses the whole frame along with lens information (color, distance) from G, E, and D lenses to determine exposure. Best for most situations.

Center-Weighted: Uses information predominantly from center of frame to determine exposure.

Spot: Uses area under current focus point to determine exposure.

Highlight-Weighted: Camera determines exposure in order to keep detail in the brightest highlights.

EXPOSURE COMPENSATION

Press Exposure Compensation button on top right of camera and turn Main Command dial to adjust exposure from –5 (darker) to +5 (lighter) in 1/3-stop increments.

Note: In Manual (M) exposure mode, Exposure Compensation will change exposure indicator but not shutter speed or aperture.

FOCUS MODES

Push Fn2 button and turn Main Command dial.

AF-S (Single AF): Focus starts when shutter release button is pressed halfway and locks when focus is achieved. Best for stationary subjects.

AF-C (Continuous AF): Focus starts when shutter release button is pressed halfway and continues to focus until photo is taken. Best for moving subjects.

AF-F (Full-Time AF): Only available in Movie mode. Focus tracks subject continuously until shutter release button is pressed halfway. Can really drain the battery.

M (Manual Focus): Focusing is accomplished by turning focusing ring on lens barrel.

AF-AREA MODES (FOCUS AREA)

Push Fn2 button and turn Sub-Command dial.

Pinpoint AF: For critical focus when AF-S (Single AF) Focus mode is used.

Single-Point AF: Uses single point for focus.

Dynamic-Area AF: User selects the focus point and camera tries to keep moving subject in focus (AF-C only).

Wide-Area AF (S): Single wide point (larger than single point) used for focusing.

Wide-Area AF (L): Single wide point (larger than Wide-Area AF [S]) used for focusing.

Auto-Area AF: Camera focuses on closest thing, but faces are given priority and camera tries to focus on people over other objects.

Note: When Auto-Area AF is selected, press OK for **Subject Tracking** and camera will track subjects moving in frame.

RELEASE MODES

Press Release mode button and select desired mode using Multi Selector, then press OK.

S (Single Frame): Takes a single shot every time shutter release is pressed.

L (Continuous Low): Takes between 1–4 frames per second (FPS) as long as you press shutter release.

H (Continuous High): Takes up to 4.5 FPS for as long as you press shutter release.

Self-Timer: When shutter release is pressed fully, camera waits a set time before taking photo. To set the delay, press the Release mode button, highlight Self-Timer using Multi Selector, then press down arrow on Multi Selector. Select desired delay and number of photos to take using Multi Selector, then press OK.

WHITE BALANCE

Press and hold the Fn1 button and rotate the Main Command dial.

The **A1 (Auto)** setting is best for most situations. White balance can be set to shift colors warmer, cooler, or keep them accurate. Other settings are all matched to different lighting types. For truest colors, pick the type of lighting being used to illuminate scene.

FILE FORMAT / IMAGE QUALITY

Press the *i* button and use the Multi Selector to select Image Quality. Then rotate the Main Command dial to select from the following options.

RAW (NEF): The RAW data from the image sensor is recorded each time a photo is taken.

RAW (NEF) / JPEG: The camera saves two files each time the shutter button is pressed: a RAW file and a JPEG file. You can decide the quality of the JPEG (fine, normal, or basic). Only the JPEG is shown during playback. Deleting the JPEG also deletes the RAW file.

JPEG: The camera saves a JPEG file each time the shutter button is pressed. You can decide the quality of the JPEG (fine, normal, or basic).

Note: The JPEG files can be saved as either regular files or compressed files (choose options marked with an asterisk in order to maximize quality).

04 OTHER HELPFUL SETTINGS

PICTURE CONTROLS

***i* Menu > Set Picture Control**

Allows you to adjust settings for JPEG images. Eight preset picture controls can all be adjusted: **A (Auto), SD (Standard), NL (Neutral), VI (Vivid), MC (Monochrome), PT (Portrait), LS (Landscape), FL (Flat),** and the custom option **01–20 (Creative Picture Control)**. You can modify the picture controls in the Manage Picture Control menu, adjusting Effect Level, Sharpness, Contrast, Brightness, Saturation, Hue, Filter Effects, and Toning. Monochrome images can have a Yellow, Orange, Red, or Green filter applied. The Creative Picture Control applies the following effects: Dream, Morning, Pop, Sunday, Somber, Dramatic, Silence, Bleached, Melancholic, Pure, Denim, Toy, Sepia, Blue, Red, Pink, Charcoal, Graphite, Binary, or Carbon.

FLASH MODES

***i* Menu > Flash Mode**

Fill Flash: The flash fires with each shot. When using P or A shooting mode, camera uses shutter speed between 1/60–1/200 sec. (1/60–1/8000 sec. when Auto FP High-Speed Sync is selected).

Red-Eye Reduction: Flash fires twice: first pre-flash burst is so that subject's pupils close, reducing the red-eye. Not good for moving subjects.

Slow Sync: Flash is used in conjunction with slower shutter speeds to allow ambient light into photo. Only available in P and A shooting modes.

Slow Sync and Red-Eye Reduction: Combines red-eye reduction pre-flash and slow sync for better portraits taken when you want ambient light in photo. Only available in P and A shooting modes.

Rear-Curtain Sync: Flash fires at end of exposure, creating more natural-looking light trails if subject is moving. Only available in S and M shooting modes. P and A shooting modes will set flash to Slow Sync.

Flash Off: Flash does not fire.

COLOR SPACE

Photo Shooting Menu > Color Space

sRGB: Smaller color space. Best when images are used directly from camera.

Adobe RGB: Larger color space. Best used when images will be edited with post-processing software.

HIGHLIGHT WARNING (BLINKIES)

Playback Menu > Playback Display Options, select Highlights

Shows pure white areas as blinking highlights on playback. Useful to know if areas are being overexposed.

NOISE REDUCTION

Photo Shooting Menu > Long Exposure NR

Reduces noise in images with shutter speeds of 1 second or longer. Doubles time needed to save image to memory card. Affects both RAW and JPEG images.

Photo Shooting Menu > High ISO NR

Reduces noise in images taken at high ISO settings. Use Normal for default, Low for less noise reduction, and High for more noise reduction. Affects only JPEG images.

AUTO ISO

Hold ISO button and rotate Sub-Command dial to turn Auto ISO on or off.

You can set the **Maximum Sensitivity** (the highest ISO the camera will use) in Photo Shooting Menu > ISO Sensitivity Settings > Maximum Sensitivity.

DISP BUTTON

Press the DISP button to cycle through the available views on the monitor and/or viewfinder.

Indicators On: Shows all the data of the scene.

Simplified Display: Shows a subset of the full info.

Histogram: Shows a live histogram.

Virtual Horizon: Shows a Virtual Horizon, allowing you to adjust the camera until it is level. Useful for shooting landscapes.

Information Display (monitor only): Shows the current camera settings.

Flash Info (monitor only): Shows the Flash settings. Available only when a compatible Nikon Speedlight is attached.

Note: When in Movie mode, the Flash Info and Information Display options are not shown.

Press the DISP button to cycle through the following screen overlays when viewing images in full-frame playback on the monitor and/or viewfinder.

File Information: Shows file name and capture data.

Exposure Data: Shows exposure data for selected image.

Highlight Display: Areas of pure white blink as a warning.

RGB Histogram: Shows histogram for current image.

Shooting Data: Shows all the shooting data for current image.

Location Data: Shows location data if embedded in image at time of capture.

Overview Data: Shows all data on single screen.

None: Shows just the image.

ACTIVE D-LIGHTING

Photo Shooting Menu > Active D-Lighting

Used to help preserve detail that can be lost in both the darkest and brightest parts of a high-contrast image. You can set the strength to Auto, Extra High, High, Normal, or Low, or you can turn Active D-Lighting off.

Note: This feature can cause image issues such as banding and noise at higher ISO settings.

BKT AUTO BRACKETING

Photo Shooting Menu > Auto Bracketing

Auto Bracketing is used to take a set of images where exposure, flash power, white balance, or Active D-Lighting is changed slightly between each frame. You can set the camera to whichever option you would like to bracket:

Exposure (AE) & Flash: Changes the exposure and the flash power.

Exposure (AE): Changes the exposure.

Flash: Changes the flash power.

WB: Changes the white balance.

ADL: Changes the amount of the Active D-Lighting applied.

You can also set the number of shots and the increment of change between each shot. For ADL bracketing, you adjust the Amount of change, not the Increment.

WIRELESS CONNECTION (SNAPBRIDGE)

Use the Nikon SnapBridge app on your smartphone or tablet to connect the Z5 to the device.

Allows for wireless downloading of images and remote control of camera via Bluetooth. The Z5 can also connect to a computer via the built-in Wi-Fi.

05 STEP-BY-STEP SHOOTING INSTRUCTIONS

MULTIPLE EXPOSURES

Create in-camera multiple exposures:

1. Select Photo Shooting Menu > Multiple Exposure, and press right on the Multi Selector.
2. Choose the Multiple Exposure mode:
   On (series): Takes multiple exposures until Off is selected.
   On (single): Takes one multiple exposure.
   Off: Turns multiple exposures off.
3. Select Number of Shots to combine.
4. Pick the Overlay mode:
   Add: The images are combined without any modification.
   Average: Before the images are combined, the gain for each image is divided by the total number of images to create a proper exposure.
   Lighten: Camera uses only lightest pixels of each image to create an overall light image.
   Darken: Camera uses only darkest pixels of each image to create an overall dark image.
5. Choose whether to keep the individual (NEF) images by selecting Save Individual Images (NEF) and choosing On or Off, then pressing OK.

6. Choose whether to view the progress in the display by selecting Overlay Shooting and choosing On or Off, then pressing OK.

7. If you want to use an existing file as the first exposure, choose Select First Exposure (NEF) and press right on the Multi Selector. Select an image from the memory card, then press OK.

Note: Multiple exposures shot with the RAW file type will be recorded as JPEG fine (compressed) format.

HDR HDR

Combine two images to reduce the contrast and improve tonal range:

1. Select Photo Shooting Menu > HDR (High Dynamic Range), and press right on the Multi Selector.

2. Choose to shoot either a series of images (On [series])—which will continue to shoot HDR until you select Off in HDR mode—or a single occurrence (On [single photo]).

3. Pick the Exposure Differential between two photos, as well as the Smoothing.

4. Choose whether to keep the individual exposures (Save Individual Images [NEF]).

5. Press the shutter release once to take both photos.

TIME-LAPSE MOVIES

Create a time-lapse movie in-camera:

1. Select Photo Shooting Menu > Time-Lapse Movie, and press right on the Multi Selector.
2. Select the Interval: the time between each photo. Set in minutes and seconds.
3. Select the Shooting Time: how long to shoot (up to 7 hours and 59 minutes).
4. Choose whether you want to use Exposure Smoothing. When On, it automatically tries to smooth any big changes in the exposure.
5. Turn Silent Photography On or Off.
6. Choose the Image Area to capture.
7. Choose the Frame Size/Frame Rate for the final output.
8. Turn Interval Priority On or Off. On ensures that frames shot in P or A mode will use the set interval even if that creates an underexposed image. When On, the time-lapse will end if the camera cannot focus.
9. Turn Focus before each shot On or Off. When On, the camera autofocuses between each shot.
10. Choose a Destination for the movie. Decide if the final movie is saved to the memory card in Slot 1 or Slot 2.
11. Select Start and press OK.

INTVL INTERVAL TIMER PHOTOGRAPHY

Set the camera to take a series of photos over a period of time:

1. Select Photo Shooting Menu > Interval Timer Shooting, and press right on the Multi Selector.
2. Set Start options to begin either in 3 seconds (Now) or at least 1 minute in future (Choose Day/Time).
3. Set the Interval between photos (Hours/Minutes/Seconds).
4. Set number of intervals and the number of shots per interval (Intervals x Shots/Interval).
5. Turn Exposure Smoothing On or Off.
6. Turn Silent Photography On or Off.
7. Turn Interval Priority On or Off. When On, photos shot in P or A mode will be taken at the chosen interval; when Off, the photos will use shutter speed to achieve proper exposure even if that is longer than the selected interval.
8. Turn Focus before each shot On or Off. When On, the camera autofocuses between each shot.
9. From the Options menu, select if you want AE Bracketing On or Off, and set the Number of Shots and Increment.
10. From the Options menu, select if you want a Time-Lapse Movie created, and choose settings for Frame Size/Frame Rate and Destination.
11. Select the Starting Storage Folder.
12. Select Start and press OK.

06 TYPICAL SHOOTING SCENARIOS

SHOOTING SCENARIO **PORTRAIT**

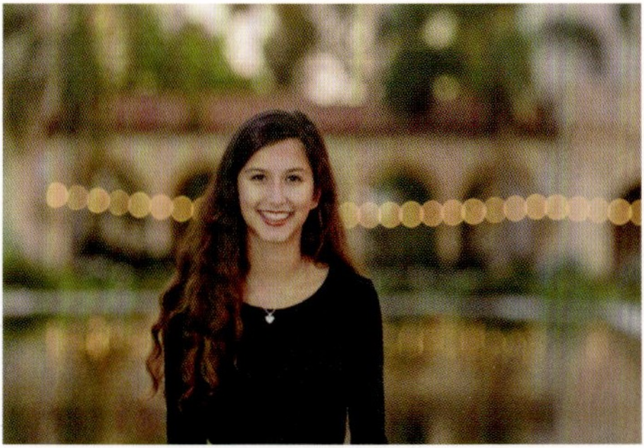

KEY PRINCIPLES

- The key to a portrait like this is shallow depth of field. So shoot in **APERTURE PRIORITY** mode and start with the lowest aperture your lens offers (such as **f/2.8 or f/4**).
- Remember to **focus on the eyes**.
- If the image is too dark or too light, use **EXPOSURE COMPENSATION** to adjust the brightness level.

- If the image is blurry from a slow shutter speed, **raise the ISO** to increase your sensor's sensitivity to light, thus allowing for a faster shutter speed.
- Remember to use a **focal length of 50mm or greater** so that you don't distort your subject's face.

SHOOTING SCENARIO
GROUP PORTRAIT

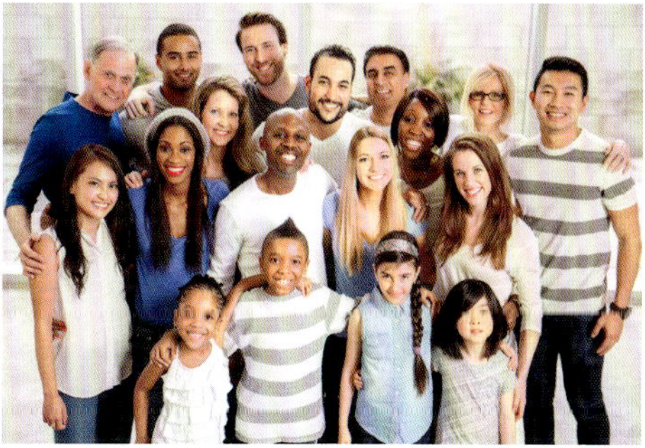

KEY PRINCIPLES

- In order to get everyone in focus, you need a deep depth of field. So shoot in **APERTURE PRIORITY** mode and set the aperture between **f/8–f/16**.

- **Focus on the person in the middle of the group**. Check focus by using the Zoom In button to view it at 100% and check faces in the front and back rows. If anyone is out of focus, use a smaller aperture for deeper depth of field.
- Use **MATRIX METERING** to account for the light in the entire scene.
- **Arrange the group so they can all see you** (and you can see them).
- Use **EXPOSURE COMPENSATION** if the image is too bright or too dark.
- If image is blurry, **raise the ISO** to allow the camera to use a faster shutter speed.

SHOOTING SCENARIO

LANDSCAPE

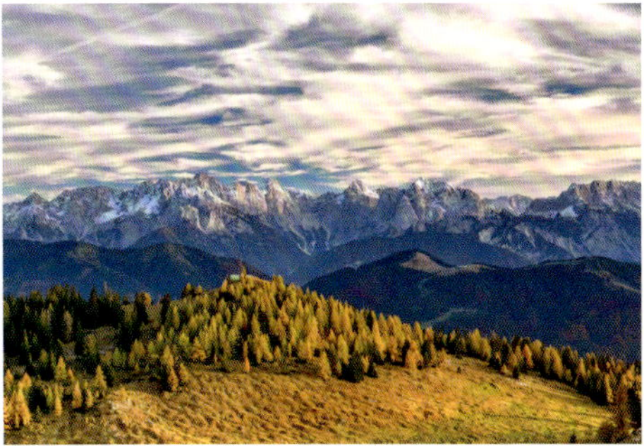

KEY PRINCIPLES

- Shoot in **APERTURE PRIORITY** to control depth of field, and start with **f/16** to ensure deep depth of field.
- **Use a tripod** to eliminate camera movement. Whenever your camera is on a tripod, also make sure that **VIBRATION REDUCTION is turned off**.
- Use **MATRIX METERING** mode and **SINGLE AUTOFOCUS (AF-S)** Focus mode.
- **Set the ISO to a low setting (100–200)** to avoid any digital noise.

- Shoot in **RAW** so that you have the most available information when editing later.
- Consider **BRACKETING** your exposures.

SHOOTING SCENARIO
FREEZE ACTION

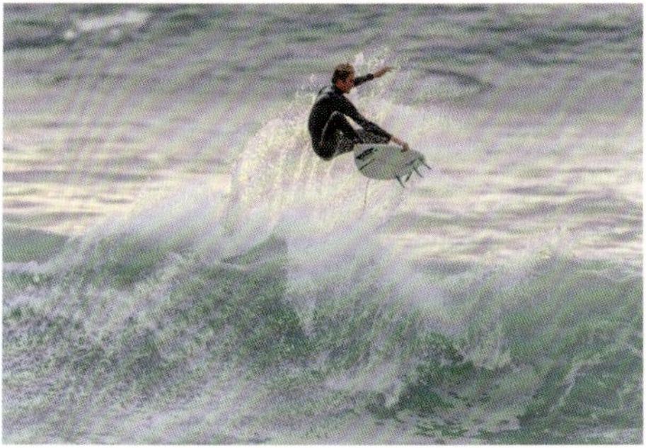

KEY PRINCIPLES

- Use **SHUTTER PRIORITY** mode and set the shutter speed to a value that will freeze the action. The appropriate shutter speed depends on your subject and its movement, but could be anywhere between **1/500–1/8000 sec**.

- Use **CONTINUOUS AUTOFOCUS (AF-C)** so that the camera keeps focusing as the subject moves.
- If the image is dark or blurry, **raise the ISO** or try AUTO ISO to automatically have the camera adjust the ISO as needed.

SHOOTING SCENARIO
SHOWING MOTION—PANNING

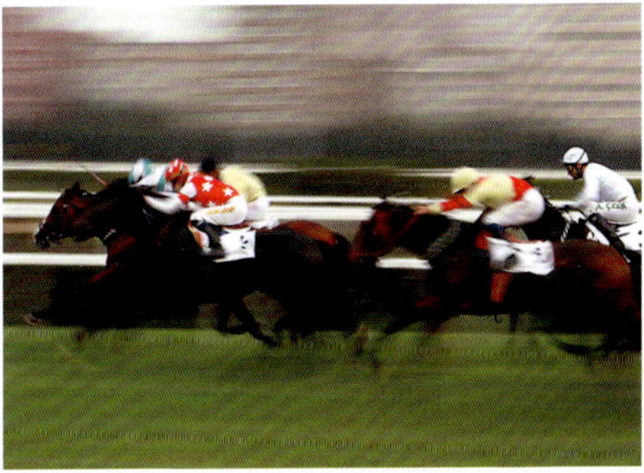

KEY PRINCIPLES

- Shoot in **SHUTTER PRIORITY** mode and use a slow-enough shutter speed to allow for the subject to move during the exposure.

- **Follow the subject** across the frame as you shoot.
- Try using **LIVE VIEW**, which allows you to see the subject during the exposure.
- Use **CONTINUOUS AUTOFOCUS (AF-C)**, as well as **DYNAMIC-AREA AF**.

SHOOTING SCENARIO
LOW-LIGHT ACTION

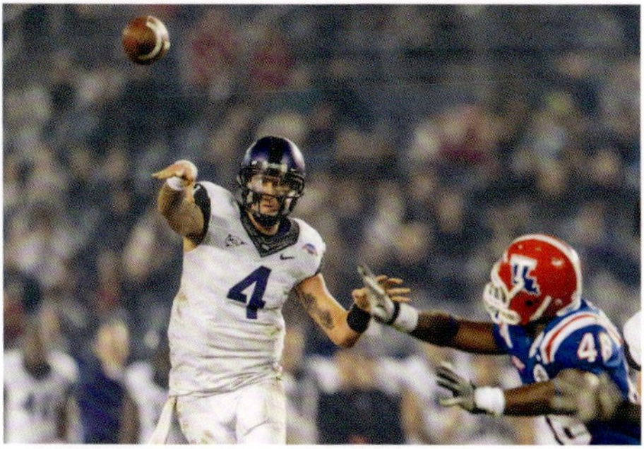

KEY PRINCIPLES

- Shoot in **APERTURE PRIORITY** mode and use a wide aperture such as **f/2.8 or f/4**.
- Use **SPOT METERING** and meter on the subject's face.

- Use **CONTINUOUS AUTOFOCUS (AF-C)** and a single AF point.
- **Set the ISO to 1600 or higher**, depending on the amount of available light.
- If the image is blurry, **increase the ISO** to allow for a faster shutter speed.

SHOOTING SCENARIO
LONG EXPOSURE

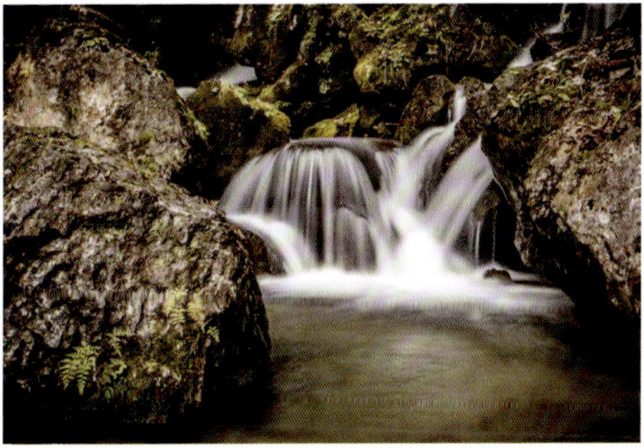

KEY PRINCIPLES

- Use **MANUAL** shooting mode, which allows you to use the **BULB** or **TIME** setting for long exposures.

- **Use a tripod** to keep the camera stable. **Turn off any VIBRATION REDUCTION feature**.
- Use the **SINGLE AUTOFOCUS (AF-S)** Focus mode, or try manual focus if the camera is having a hard time locking on focus.
- **Use a low ISO** (100–400) and **shoot RAW** to ensure a high-quality file.
- Use a **remote release cord** with a lock to avoid touching (shaking) the camera.

7. **Movie Shooting Button:** Press to start and stop movie recording.
8. **Multi-Function/FTP Server Image Transfer Button:** Press this button to initiate an FTP transfer from the camera.
9. **Shutter Release Button:** Press to focus and press all the way down to take photos.
10. **Main Dial:** Used to change settings.
11. **Power/Multi-Function Lock Switch:** Turns camera on and off/ Locks the Multi-Function switch.
12. **Mode Button:** Used to change modes.
13. **Quick Control Dial 2:** Used to change settings.

CAMERA BODY BACK

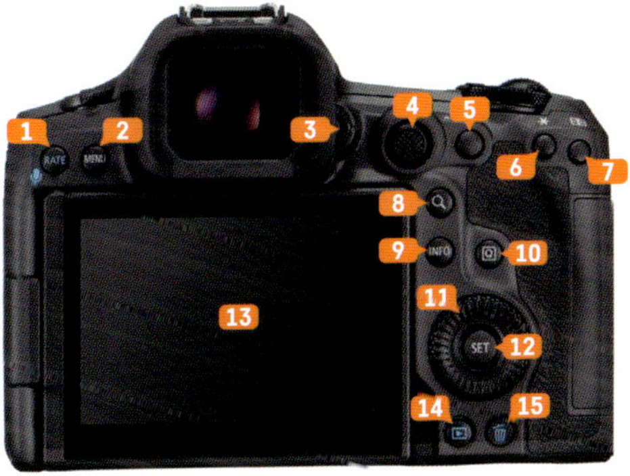

1. **Rating/Voice Memo Button:** Set photo rating/Use to attach voice memo to image.
2. **MENU Button:** Use to access the camera's menu system.
3. **Diopter Adjustment:** Adjust the diopter of the viewfinder.

4. **Multi-Controller:** Used to navigate settings.
5. **AF-ON Button:** Turns the autofocus on.
6. **AE Lock Button:** Used to lock the exposure.
7. **AF Point Selection Button:** Used to pick the desired focus point.
8. **Magnify/Reduce Button:** Used to zoom in/out of images.
9. **Info Button:** Used to open and cycle through Info displays.
10. **Quick Control Button:** Used to access the Quick Control settings.
11. **Quick Control Dial 1:** Used to make changes to selected settings.
12. **Set Button:** Used to set menu choices and other settings.
13. **Monitor:** High-resolution screen used for playback, menus, and live views.
14. **Playback Button:** Used to play back photos/videos.
15. **Trash Button:** Used to delete unwanted files.

CAMERA BODY FRONT

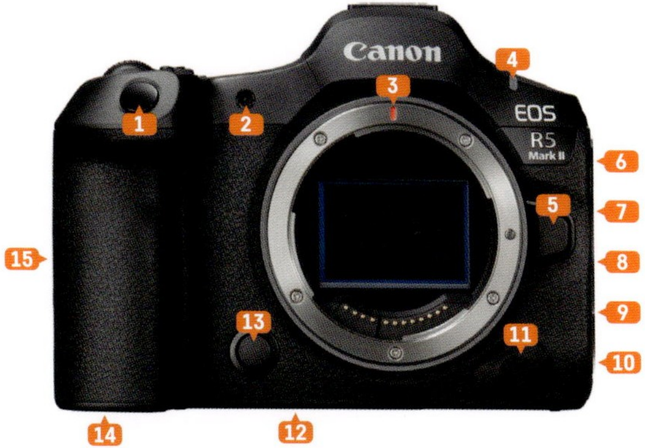

1. **Shutter Release Button:** Press to focus and press all the way down to take photos.
2. **Self-Timer Lamp/AF-Assist Beam:** Lights up when using the self-timer/Used in dark environments to help with autofocus.
3. **RF Lens Mount Index:** Used to align the lens when mounting it on the camera.
4. **Tally Lamp:** Indicates camera's status when recording movies. Lit solid: Movie recording is in progress. Blinking rapidly: Movie recording cannot proceed because of low battery, low card space, or overheating. Blinking slowly: Movie recording possible for up to 6 minutes.
5. **Lens Release Button:** Used to unlock the lens when removing it from the camera.
6. **Mic (On Side):** External microphone in terminal.
7. **USB Digital Terminal (On Side):** Port used for digital transfer.
8. **Headphone Terminal (On Side):** Used to connect headphones.
9. **HDMI Out Terminal (On Side):** Used to connect to a HDMI device.
10. **Flash Sync Terminal (On Side):** Used to connect a flash sync cable.
11. **Remote Control Terminal (Under Cover):** Used to connect a remote control to the camera.
12. **Tripod Socket (On Bottom):** Threaded socket for tripod or monopod.
13. **Depth of Field Preview Button:** Press to see what the current depth of field looks like.
14. **Battery Compartment (On Bottom):** Insert battery here.
15. **Memory Card Slots (On Side):** Insert memory cards here.

SHOOTING SCREEN (STILL PHOTO)

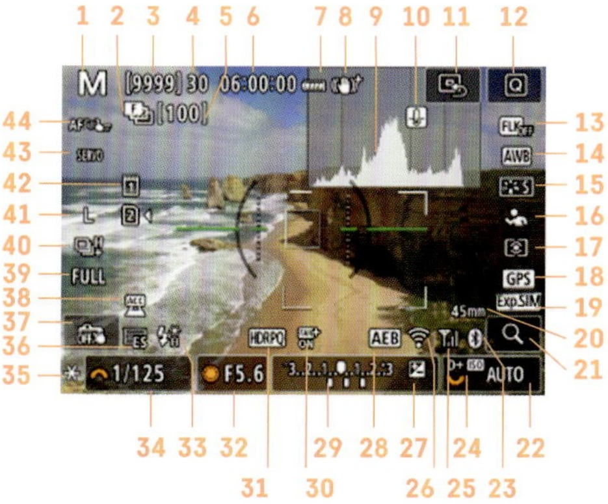

1. Shooting Mode
2. Focus Bracketing/Multiple Exposures/Bulb Timer/ Pre-Continuous/Interval Timer
3. No. of Available Shots/Sec. Until Self-Timer Shoots
4. Maximum Burst
5. No. of Remaining Shots for Focus Bracketing, Multiple Exposures, or Interval Timer
6. Movie Recording Time Available
7. Battery Level
8. Image Stabilizer (IS Mode)
9. Histogram
10. Still Photo Image Quality Warning
11. Set AF Point to Center
12. Quick Control Button

13. Anti-Flicker Shooting
14. White Balance/White Balance Correction
15. Picture Style
16. Subject to Detect
17. Metering Mode
18. GPS Connection Status
19. Display Simulation/OVF Sim. View Assist
20. Focal Length
21. Magnify Button
22. ISO Speed
23. Bluetooth Function
24. Highlight Tone Priority
25. Wi-Fi Signal Strength
26. Wi-Fi Function
27. Exposure Compensation
28. AEB/FEB
29. Exposure Level Indicator (Exposure Compensation Amount/AEB Range)
30. Cooling Fan Setting
31. HDR Shooting (PQ)/View Assist
32. Aperture Value
33. Flash Ready/FE Lock/High-Speed Sync
34. Shutter Speed/Multi-Function Lock Warning
35. AE Lock
36. Electronic Shutter
37. Touch Shutter/Create Folder
38. Accessory Attached Indicator
39. Still Photo Cropping/Aspect Ratio
40. Drive Mode
41. Image Quality
42. Card
43. AF Operation
44. AF Area

RECORDING SCREEN (MOVIE)

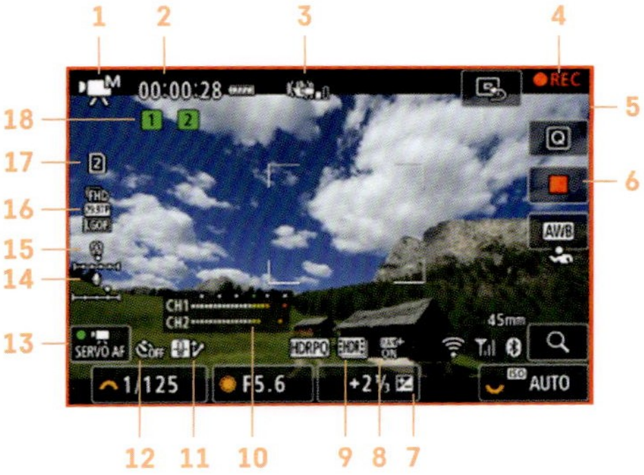

1. Shooting Mode
2. Movie Recording Time Available
3. Image Stabilizer (Movie Digital IS)
4. Movie Shooting Button (Start Recording)
5. Red Border Movie Recording in Progress
6. Movie Shooting Button (Stop Recording)
7. Exposure Level Indicator (Metering Levels)
8. Cooling Fan Settings
9. HDR Movie Recording
10. Audio Recording Level Indicator
11. Overheat Control
12. Movie Self-Timer
13. Movie Servo AF
14. Audio Recording Level (Manual Input)
15. Headphone Volume
16. Movie Recording Size

17. Card for Recording/Playback
18. Recording Status (Left: Main Movie; Right: Proxy Movie)

PLAYBACK SCREEN (STILL PHOTO)

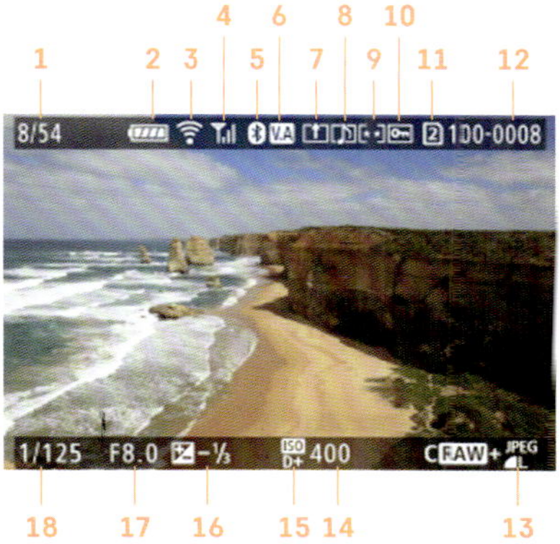

1. Current Image No./Total Images/No. of Images Found
2. Battery Level
3. Wi-Fi Function/Wired LAN
4. Wireless Signal Strength
5. Bluetooth Function
6. HDR View Assist
7. Already Sent to a Computer/Smartphone
8. Voice Memo
9. Rating
10. Image Protection

11. Card No.
12. Folder No./File No.
13. Image Quality/Edited Image/Cropping/Frame Grab
14. ISO Speed
15. Highlight Tone Priority
16. Exposure Compensation Amount
17. Aperture Value
18. Shutter Speed

PLAYBACK SCREEN (MOVIE)

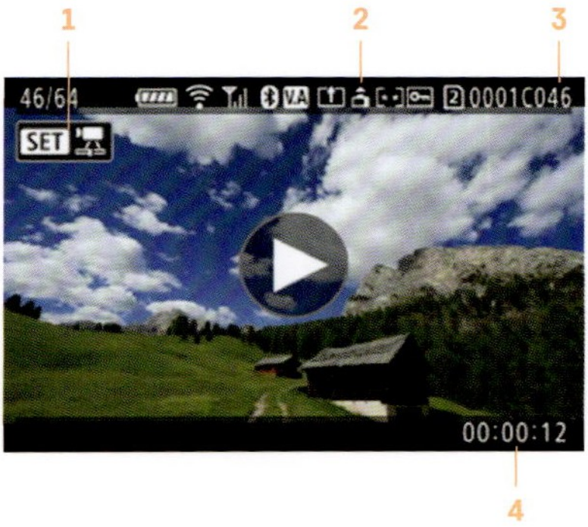

1. Movie Playback
2. Movie Orientation Information
3. Reel and Clip Numbers
4. Recording Time/Timecode

03 ESSENTIAL MODES AND SETTINGS

SHOOTING MODES

Press the Mode button and rotate Quick Control Dial 1 or 2 to select the desired shooting mode.

A+ (Scene Intelligent Auto): The camera assesses the scene and sets the optimum settings automatically. It will even adjust the focus on both still and moving subjects.

Fv (Flexible-Priority AE): Shutter speed, aperture, and ISO are all set automatically, then you can change one, two, or all three settings to get the desired exposure. Use Quick Control Dial 2 to select the setting you want to change, then use the Main dial to change it. The settings you don't change will automatically be adjusted by the camera.

P (Program AE): The camera sets the shutter speed and aperture based on metering info and current ISO.

Tv (Time Value or Shutter Speed Priority): You set the shutter speed and the camera sets the aperture based on metering info and current ISO.

Av (Aperture Value, or Aperture Priority): You set the aperture, and the camera sets the shutter speed based on metering info and current ISO.

M (Manual): You set ISO, shutter speed (Main dial), and aperture (Quick Control Dial 1). Refer to the exposure level indicator.

Bulb: Used for long exposures, the shutter stays open as long as you hold down the Shutter button. Use the Main dial to set the aperture.

C1, C2, C3 (Custom Shooting Modes): Use the Set-Up menu to set a custom shooting mode.

METERING MODES

Press the Multi-Function button, then use Quick Control Dial 1 or 2 to navigate to and select a Metering mode; or, choose Menu > Shooting (Screen 2) > Metering Mode.

Evaluative: General-purpose mode suited for most situations and subjects (even backlit subjects).

Partial: Uses 5.8% of the area at the center of the screen for determining exposure. Good choice when there is very bright light around the subject.

Spot: Uses 2.9% of the area at the center of the screen. Use when you need to meter on a specific part of the scene.

Center-Weighted Average: The camera analyzes the whole scene to determine exposure, but places more emphasis on info at the center of the screen.

EXPOSURE COMPENSATION

Press the Shutter button halfway down, then rotate Quick Control Dial 1 to adjust exposure compensation.

When shooting in the Fv shooting mode, you set the exposure compensation by rotating Quick Control Dial 2 to select the Exposure Level indicator, then using the Main dial or Quick Control Dial 1 to set the exposure compensation. To reset the exposure compensation back to 0, press the Erase/Trash button.

Note: The exposure compensation you set will remain in effect until you change it; it does not return to 0 when the camera is turned off.

FOCUS OPERATION

MENU > AF (Screen 1) > AF Operation

One Shot AF: Focus starts when the Shutter button is pressed halfway, then locks when focus is achieved. Best for stationary subjects.

AI Focus: Automatically switches between One Shot AF and Servo based on the movement of the subject when focusing.

Servo: Focus starts when the Shutter button is pressed halfway and continues to focus until photo is taken. Best for moving subjects.

Note: For **Manual focus**, set the AF/MF switch on the lens to MF and rotate the focus ring on the lens barrel to focus. Alternately, set the focus mode to MF in the Focus Mode menu.

AUTOFOCUS AREA

MENU > AF (Screen 1) > AF Method

Spot AF: The camera focuses on the smallest possible area, even narrower than 1-Point AF.

1-Point AF: The camera focuses using a single point for critical focus.

Expand AF Area: The camera uses one AF point, as well as the points adjacent and nearby to that focus point to help focus. Helpful for moving subjects that are difficult to track with 1-Point AF.

Expand AF Area: Around: The camera creates an even larger area around one AF point to find focus.

Flexible Zone AF 1-3: User-defined focus areas. The default for area 1 is a square, area 2 is a vertical rectangle, and area 3 is a horizontal rectangle.

Whole Area AF: Uses the entire frame to focus. When you press the Shutter button halfway down, all the focus points in use will have a square around them.

Whole Area Tracking Servo AF: This uses Whole Area AF to track subjects across the frame. You can choose from the following: Automatic, People, Animals, Vehicles, or none.

ADDITIONAL AUTOFOCUS OPTIONS

Move the AF point or Zone AF frame: Press the AF Point Selection button, then use the Multi-Controller to move the point to the desired location and press the Set button. To center the AF point, press the Multi-Controller straight in. You can also tap directly on the screen to select the focus point

Eye Detection: MENU > AF (Screen 2) > Eye Detection. Select Auto to have the camera automatically attempt to find focus directly on the subject's eyes when the AF method is set to

Whole Area Tracking Servo AF. You can choose which eye the camera prioritizes.

Manual Focus Peaking: MENU > AF (Screen 6) > MF Peaking Settings. When manually focusing, focus peaking informs you that focus has been achieved by lighting up when edges of subject are in focus.

DRIVE MODES

Press the M-Fn (Multi-Function) button and rotate Quick Control Dial 1 to select the Drive Mode option, then rotate the Main dial to select the desired mode.

Single Shooting: The camera takes a single shot every time Shutter button is fully pressed.

High-Speed Continuous Shooting +: The camera takes up to 12 frames per second when you press and hold the Shutter button using the mechanical shutter and the electronic 1st-curtain shutter. You can take 30 shots per second when using the electronic shutter.

High-Speed Continuous Shooting: The camera takes up to 6 frames per second when using the mechanical shutter when you press and hold the Shutter button and 8.2 shots per second using the electronic 1st-curtain shutter. You can take 15 shots per second when using the electronic shutter.

Low-Speed Continuous Shooting: The camera takes up to 3 frames per second when you press and hold the Shutter button. You can take 5 shots per second when using the electronic shutter.

Self-Timer 10: Sets the self-timer for 10 seconds.

Self-Timer 2: Sets the self-timer for 2 seconds.

Self-Timer: Continuous shooting: The camera waits 10 seconds then takes the selected number of photos.

SHUTTER MODE

MENU > Shooting (screen 6) > Shutter Mode

Mechanical: Uses the mechanical shutter, recommended when shooting wide open with fast glass.

Electronic 1st-Curtain: The front curtain opens silently; taking the photos uses the mechanical rear curtain.

Electronic: This uses the electronic curtain for the whole photograph with no shutter noise and less vibration

WHITE BALANCE

Press the Quick Control menu then navigate to the White Balance setting or use Menu > Shooting Menu (Screen 4) > White Balance.

Auto (AWB) (Ambience Priority) is best for most situations. **AWB-W** (White Priority) is best when you want to reduce a warm color cast. White balance can be set to shift colors warmer, cooler, or keep them accurate. Other settings are all matched to different lighting types. For truest colors, pick the type of lighting being used to illuminate the scene.

IMAGE QUALITY

MENU > Shooting (Screen 1) > Image Quality. Use the Main dial to select the RAW quality, and use Quick Control Dial 1 to select the JPEG quality.

RAW/C-RAW (Compact RAW): The RAW data from the image sensor is recorded each time a photo is taken. The C-RAW version is a compressed RAW file that takes up less space.

RAW/JPEG: If you have selected both a RAW and JPEG option, the camera saves two files each time the Shutter button is pressed: a RAW file and a JPEG file. You also decide the size of the JPEG (fine, normal, large, medium, small).

JPEG: The camera saves a JPEG file each time the Shutter button is pressed. You also decide the size of the JPEG.

HEIF: This file type is used for HDR photography and can be converted to JPEG after shooting.

04 OTHER HELPFUL SETTINGS

PICTURE STYLES

MENU > Shooting (Screen 3) > Picture Style

You can pick one of seven preset picture controls that can all be adjusted: **A (Auto)**, **S (Standard)**, **P (Portrait)**, **L (Landscape)**, **FD (Fine Detail)**, **N (Neutral)**, **F (Faithful)**, **M (Monochrome)**, and **User Defined 1–3**.

The following settings can be adjusted for each Picture Style: **Sharpness** (Strength, Fineness, Threshold), **Contrast**, **Saturation**, **Color Tone**, **Filter Effect** (Monochrome), and **Toning Effect** (Monochrome).

User Defined: Select a User Defined slot 1–3, then press the Info button. Select Picture Style and press Set, then select a new base Picture Style and press Set. You can now adjust the individual settings. Press the MENU button to save the adjusted setting.

CUSTOM WHITE BALANCE

Setting a custom White Balance can help you get the best color when you're shooting under mixed lighting:

1. Press the Quick Control button, then select White Balance.

2. Select [Custom], then select the number of the Custom White Balance you want to set (1–5).

3. Take a photo of a white card (or white wall) under the mixed lighting at the scene. Be sure to fill the screen (this may require you to switch to manual focus to create the exposure).

COLOR SPACE

MENU > Shooting (Screen 3) > Color Space

sRGB: Smaller color space. Best when images are used directly from camera. When using A+ (Scene Intelligent Auto) shooting mode, the color space is automatically set to sRGB.

Adobe RGB: Larger color space. Best used when images will be edited with post-processing software.

HIGHLIGHT ALERT (BLINKIES)

MENU > Playback (Screen 4) > Highlight Alert

When enabled, clipped highlights will blink during image playback, alerting you to possible overexposure. To obtain more detail in those areas, adjust the exposure settings or exposure compensation and shoot again.

NOISE REDUCTION

MENU > Shooting (Screen 4) > Long Exposure Noise Reduction

Reduces noise in images with shutter speeds of 1 second or longer. Doubles the time needed to save the image to the memory card. Choices are Auto, Enable, and Disable. Auto is usually the best choice.

MENU > Shooting (Screen 4) > High ISO Speed NR

Reduces noise in images taken at high ISO settings. Use Standard for default, Low for less noise reduction, and High for more noise reduction. Set to Disable to turn noise reduction off.

EXPOSURE BRACKETING

You can bracket a set of three exposures up to +/–3 stops in 1/3-stop increments:

1. Select MENU > Shooting (Screen 2) > Exposure Compensation/AEB.
2. Set the Bracketing Range by turning the Main dial.

3. If desired, set the exposure compensation amount by turning Quick Control Dial 1. Press Set.

4. Take the pictures, and the bracketed sequence will be created. (If you're in Single shooting drive mode, take three pictures to create the bracketed sequence. If you're in a Continuous shooting drive mode, the three shots will be taken together when you press and hold the Shutter button.)

Note: Bracketing will remain on until you set the Bracketing Range back to 0.

WIRELESS CONNECTION TO SMARTPHONE OR TABLET

Turn on Bluetooth on both the camera and the device. A QR code will appear on the camera when paired to allow you to download the latest version of the necessary software. Download and install the software on the device.

1. Select MENU > Communication Functions (Screen 2) > Connect to smartphone (tablet).

2. Enable network. (This screen will not appear if the network is already enabled.)

3. Select Camera Connect, then click Add a Device to connect to it.

4. Enable Bluetooth. (This screen will not appear if Bluetooth is already enabled.)

5. If the camera is already connected to a device, it will ask if you want to disconnect that device first.

6. The QR code needed to download the latest software will appear. Press Set to start pairing. Open the app on your device to continue paring.

This will allow you to view and transfer images to your smartphone, see the Live View image on your smartphone, and even shoot remotely from your smartphone.

RESET CAMERA

MENU > Set-Up (Screen 5) > Reset Camera

Select Factory Reset to reset all settings to factory defaults and reset individual settings to choose which settings to restore to factory default.

05 STEP-BY-STEP SHOOTING INSTRUCTIONS

MULTIPLE EXPOSURES

Create in-camera multiple exposures:

1. Select MENU > Shooting (Screen 5) > Multiple Exposure.
2. Choose a shooting option:

   Disable: Turns Multiple Exposure off.

   On: Function/Control: Choose this if you want to shoot gradually and check the results as you shoot.

   On: Continuous Shooting: Choose this if you're shooting continuous multiple exposures of moving subjects.
3. Choose a Multiple Exposure Control option:

   Additive: The exposure of each image is added cumulatively.

   Average: Based on the number of exposures you set (next step), negative exposure compensation is added automatically as you shoot to achieve a standard overall exposure.

   Bright: Retains brightest portion of images.

   Dark: Retains darkest portion of images.
4. Set the number of exposures you'd like to combine, then press Set.

5. Specify whether you'd like to save all the individual images or just the resulting multiple exposure.

6. Set a Continue Multiple Exposure option:

   1-Shot Only: Shoot just one multiple exposure.

   Continuously: Continue shooting multiple exposures until you disable the feature.

7. Shoot all of the exposures to combine into one multiple exposure.

Note: When shooting using the Function/Control method (step 2), press the Playback button after taking individual shots for additional options (such as deleting the previous image so you can recapture a shot).

FOCUS BRACKETING

Combine multiple images with slightly different focus points into a single image:

1. Select MENU > Shooting (Screen 5) > Focus Bracketing.
2. Select Enable to turn it on and Disable to turn it off.
3. Select the number of shots to combine (2–999).
4. Set the focus increment. This determines how much the camera adjusts the focus between shots.

5. Turn exposure smoothing on or off.

6. Enable or disable depth composite. When enabled, both the depth composite image and the source images are saved.

7. Enable or disable crop depth compositing: When enabled, the camera crops each image to make sure the final image has the proper angle of view.

8. Set the flash interval: When set to zero, the camera takes the photo and the flash fires as soon as it's able.

9. Take the photos.

TIME-LAPSE MOVIES

Create a time-lapse movie in-camera:

1. Select MENU > Shooting (Screen 5) > Time-Lapse Movie, and choose Enable.

2. Select Interval and enter both the shooting duration and the movie duration.

3. Set the Number of Shots you'd like to take for the time-lapse movie.

4. Select the desired Movie Recording Size (4K or Full HD) and the Main Recording Format (10 bit or 8 bit).

5. Select Auto Exposure to choose the shooting method:

Fixed 1st Frame: The first shot is metered, then all subsequent shots match that first shot's exposure.

Each Frame: Each frame is metered and shot separately.

6. In the Screen Auto Off option, choose Disable to have the image displayed (though the screen will automatically turn off 30 minutes after the time-lapse shooting begins); choose Enable to have the screen turn off 10 seconds after the time-lapse shooting begins.

Note: You can press the INFO button at any time during time-lapse shooting to turn on and off the screen.

7. Choose whether you'd like to hear a beep after every image is captured (choose Beep as Image Taken). Set to 0 for no beep.

8. Once all these settings are selected, press MENU to turn off the menu screen.

9. A message will come on screen prompting you to take a test shot. Press OK, and take a test shot or two to make sure the correct focus and exposure are set.

10. Press the Movie Shooting button, then press the Shutter button to start shooting the time-lapse movie.

06 TYPICAL SHOOTING SCENARIOS

SHOOTING SCENARIO
PORTRAIT

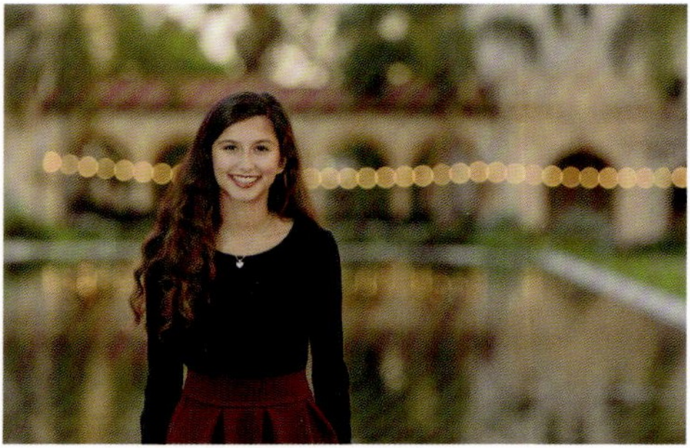

KEY PRINCIPLES

- The key to a portrait like this is shallow depth of field. So, shoot in **APERTURE PRIORITY (Av)** mode and start with the lowest aperture your lens offers (such as **f/2.8** or **f/4**).
- Remember to **focus on the eyes**.

- If the image is too dark or too light, use **EXPOSURE COMPENSATION** to adjust the brightness level.
- If the image is blurry from a slow shutter speed, **raise the ISO** to increase your sensor's sensitivity to light, thus allowing for a faster shutter speed.
- Remember to use a **focal length of 50mm or greater** so that you don't distort your subject's face.

SHOOTING SCENARIO
GROUP PORTRAIT

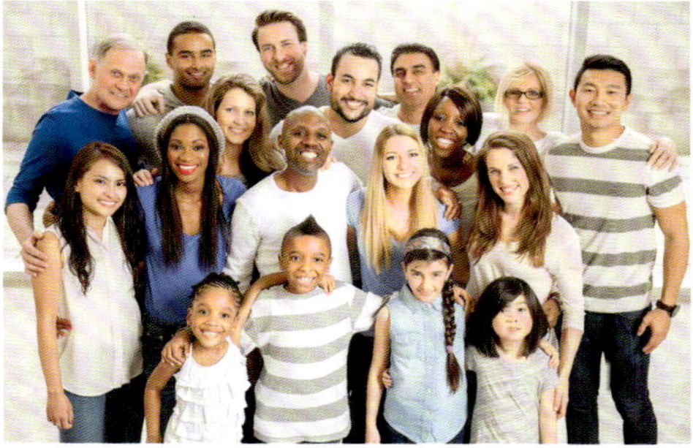

KEY PRINCIPLES

- In order to get everyone in focus, you need a deep depth of field. So, shoot in **APERTURE PRIORITY (Av)** mode and set the aperture between **f/8–f/16**.
- **Focus on the person in the middle of the group**. Check the focus by using the LCD screen. View it at 100%, and check faces in the front and back rows. If anyone is out of focus, use a smaller aperture for deeper depth of field.
- Use **EVALUATIVE METERING** to account for the light in the entire scene.
- **Arrange the group so they can all see you** (and you can see them).
- Use **EXPOSURE COMPENSATION** if the image is too bright or too dark.
- If image is blurry, **raise the ISO** to allow the camera to use a faster shutter speed.

SHOOTING SCENARIO

LANDSCAPE

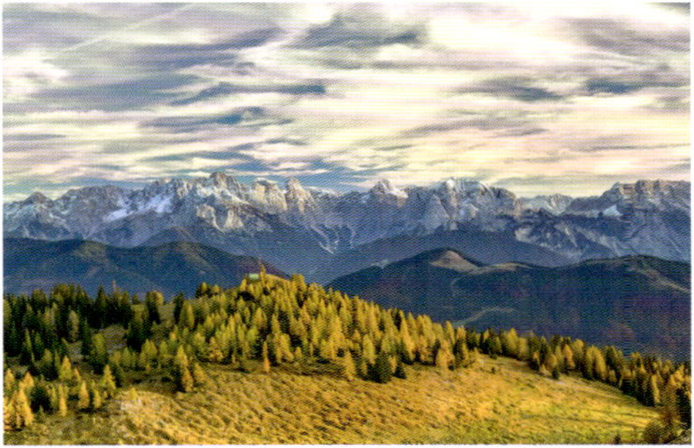

KEY PRINCIPLES

- Shoot in **APERTURE PRIORITY (Av) mode** to control depth of field, and start with **f/16** to ensure deep depth of field
- **Use a tripod** to eliminate camera movement. Whenever your camera is on a tripod, also make sure that any **IMAGE STABILIZATION** is turned off.
- Use **EVALUATIVE METERING** and **ONE SHOT AF** focus mode.
- **Set the ISO to a low setting (100–200)** to avoid any digital noise.

- Shoot in **RAW** so that you have the most available information when editing later.
- Consider **BRACKETING** your exposures.

SHOOTING SCENARIO
FREEZE ACTION

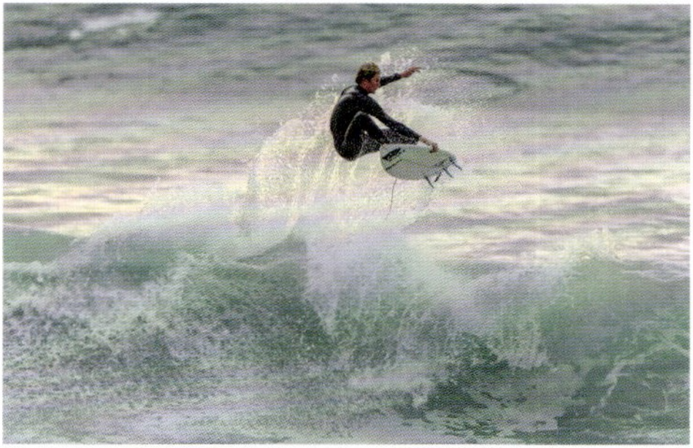

KEY PRINCIPLES

- Use **SHUTTER PRIORITY (Tv)** mode and set the shutter speed to a value that will freeze the action. The appropriate shutter speed depends on your subject and its movement, but could be anywhere between **1/500–1/8000 sec**.

- Use **SERVO** autofocus so that the camera keeps focusing as the subject moves.
- If the image is dark or blurry, **raise the ISO or try AUTO ISO** to automatically have the camera adjust the ISO as needed.

SHOOTING SCENARIO
SHOWING MOTION—PANNING

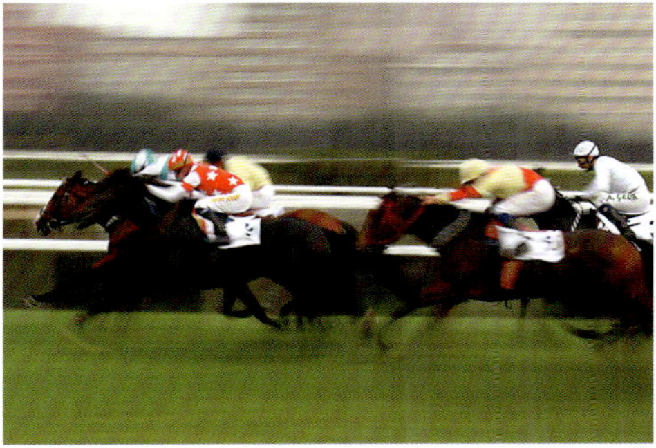

KEY PRINCIPLES

- Shoot in **SHUTTER PRIORITY (Tv)** mode and use a slow enough shutter speed to allow for the subject to move during the exposure.

- **Follow the subject** across the frame as you shoot.
- Use **SERVO** autofocus, as well as the **EXPAND AF AREA** focus mode to ensure the camera focuses on the subject.

SHOOTING SCENARIO
LOW-LIGHT ACTION

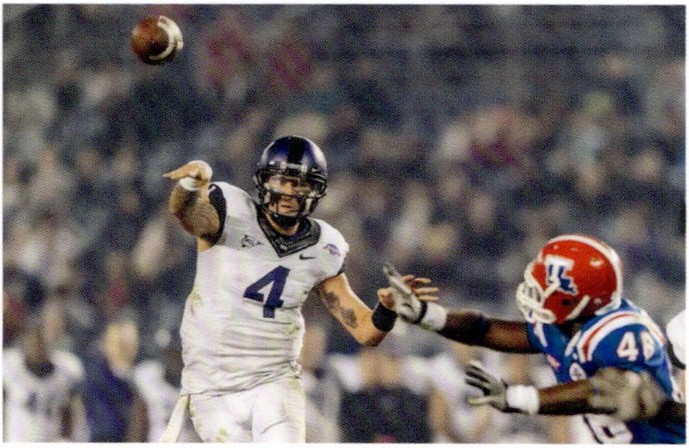

KEY PRINCIPLES

- Shoot in **APERTURE PRIORITY (Av)** mode and use a wide aperture such as **f/2.8** or **f/4**.
- Use **PARTIAL METERING** and meter on the subject's face.
- Use **SERVO** autofocus and **1-POINT AF** (a single focus point).

- **Set the ISO to 1600 or higher**, depending on the amount of available light.
- If the image is blurry, **increase the ISO** to allow for a faster shutter speed.

SHOOTING SCENARIO

LONG EXPOSURE

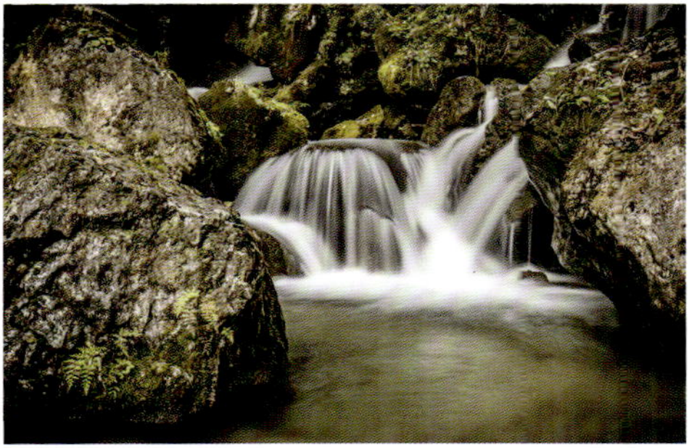

KEY PRINCIPLES

- Use **MANUAL** or **BULB** shooting mode so you can use a long shutter speed.
- **Use a tripod** to keep the camera stable. **Turn off any IMAGE STABILIZATION**.

- Use the **ONE SHOT AF** focus mode, or try manual focus if the camera is having a hard time locking on focus.
- **Use a low ISO** (100–400) and **shoot RAW** to ensure a high-quality file.
- Use a **cable release** with a lock to avoid touching (shaking) the camera.

SHOOTING SCENARIO
MACRO/CLOSE-UP

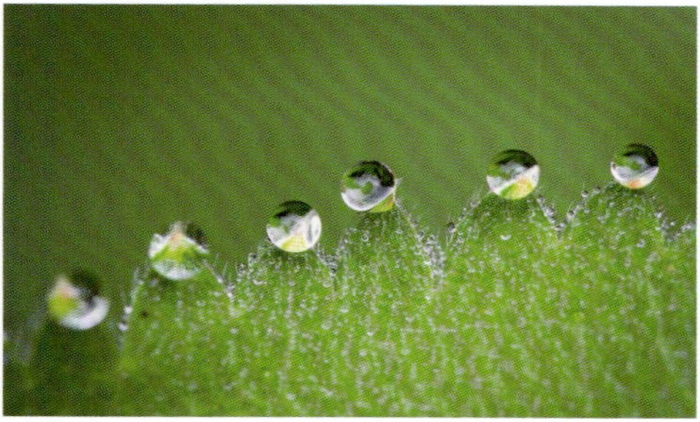

KEY PRINCIPLES

- Shoot in **APERTURE PRIORITY (Av)** mode and **use a small aperture** to ensure you achieve enough depth of field (this image was shot at f/13).

- Use **EVALUATIVE METERING** to analyze the light in the entire frame.
- A **tripod** is very useful for keeping the camera steady.
- Use **MANUAL FOCUS** and **zoom in** to confirm your focus is tack-sharp.
- Try using a dedicated **macro lens** or **close-up filters** to make sure you can achieve sharp focus when you're so close to the subject.

SHOOTING SCENARIO
VIDEO RECORDING/VLOGGING

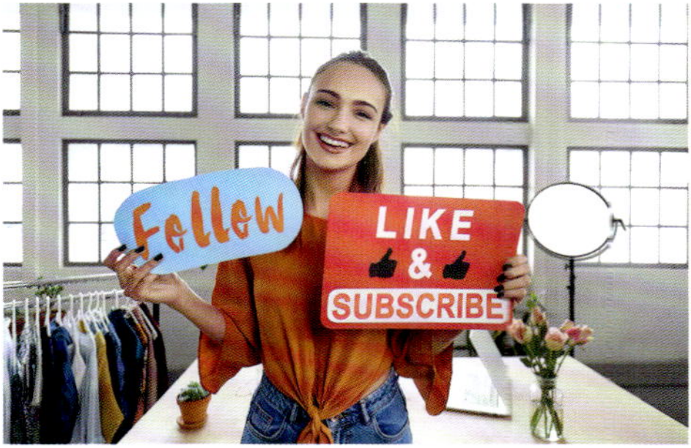

KEY PRINCIPLES

- Use a **shallow depth of field** to keep the viewers' attention on the subject. A **wide aperture** will keep the subject in focus while having the area in front of and behind the subject fall out of focus.
- Use **24 fps** for a more cinematic look.
- Set the **shutter speed** to **twice the frame rate**, or as close as you can get. If using 24 fps, the shutter speed should be 1/50 (or 1/60) second.
- Use an **external microphone** for better sound. The Rode VideoMic GO II is a great starter microphone.
- Keep the camera stable with a **tripod or gimble**. Smooth footage looks more professional.
- Use the **swing-out monitor** to watch the video being recorded. Remember to leave 1 or 2 seconds of nothing at the beginning and end of your video clips—this will make them much easier to edit later.